Your Compass to the Light:
A Practical Guide to Nourishing Your Light and Power in Challenging Times

Animamio
PRESS

Animamio Press
www.animamio.com
animamiopress@gmail.com

Table of Contents

Dedication

"The old world is dying, and the new world struggles to be born: Now is the time of monsters."
– **Antonio Gramsci**

To all those brave souls battling monsters lurking out in the world and in their own shadows. Keep up the good fight.

Foreword

This little book was originally conceived as a workshop. The workshop was held virtually to a class of counsellors in Italy who wanted to explore new approaches to helping their clients during the pandemic. From their feedback and enthusiasm was born the idea to of writing the contents of that workshop into a little book. It seemed like there was a need for meaningful reflections and practices that could sustain people through uncertain, and sometimes frightening, times.

This book does not aspire to be either revolutionary or original, as we understand the word today. However, the etymology of the word original means "to go back to the beginning", "the source"; in this sense the book is "original". The concepts, practices and teachings presented in this book have deep roots in the philosophy, wisdom and metaphysics of many traditions. The Renaissance philosophers were wont to say: "Nothing new under the sun". These teachings survive, and have stood the test of time, because they speak to the fundamental nature in all of us. The great minds of the past gave us teachings that are still relevant today, and I have attempted to present them in a modern light that makes them accessible to today's reader. The chapters here represent a selection of qualities and practices that will sustain you mentally, emotionally and spiritually, and allow you to practice deep self-care. Every time we consciously engage in nurturing ourselves, our ability to care for and help others also increases. It is a profound fallacy that we can love others while failing to love and care for ourselves. You cannot draw water from an empty well.

Like any author, I present the fruits of my learning, understanding and even my life's experiences. I have found these teachings to be helpful, if not essential, to remaining grounded and hopeful in these times we live in.

Wherever you are and at whatever point you are in your life, it cannot have escaped you that we live in a challenging epoch. The rapid advance of technology, political and social upheaval, religious and racial division has left us all looking for points of reference that can give us a sense of meaning and even inner peace.

The tools I offer here are offered as aids to forge a path through the onslaught of modern-day life. I hope they speak to you as they have, over the decades, spoken to me. Nevertheless, I wanted to keep the book short, so each subject is open to further inquiry and study. Each subject matter of the following chapters could fill volumes or even entire libraries, and have done so in centuries past. For this reason, I give suggestions for further reading along the way

I have always shied away from dogma, so I present these teachings as possibilities. They are neither exhaustive nor the only ones available. If they do not speak to you, please set them aside and continue your search for practices that resonate with you. Nothing in this book is offered as an absolute truth; I don't believe dogma is at all helpful in these times. Instead, it is empowering to become the captain of your ship, which is your life. This will truly give you the ability to navigate the seas ahead and hopefully enjoy the journey as well.

The image of a compass guiding you to your light is a metaphor for activating, protecting and nurturing our inner light, intended as our inner core, our inner clarity, our personal quest as well as an act of quiet rebellion.

I have tried to keep this little book practical, because, in my experience, you learn best through personal experience and experimentation. So each chapter strives to offer theory as well as practical and soulful tools.

Many times in my life I have picked up a book and found one word, one thought or one phrase in it that was something I needed in that given moment.

So my wish, dear reader, is that there may be one thing, however small, among these pages, that can help, inspire or comfort you on your journey.

May your path be rich in curiosity, courage and creativity.

Adrienne Prince
New Mexico, 2025

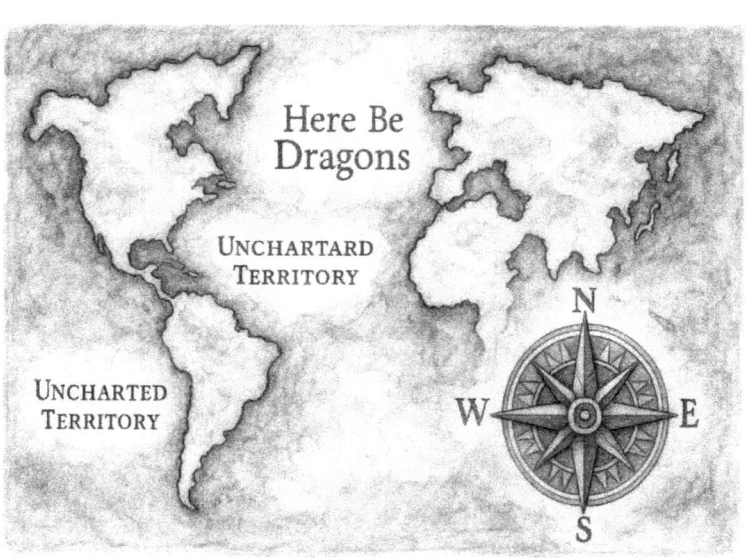

Chapter 1: The Art of Navigating Uncertainty

Wayfinding in the Unknown

"The quest for certainty blocks the search for meaning. Uncertainty is the very condition to impel man to unfold his powers." – Erich Fromm

"The only way to make sense of change is to plunge into it, move with it, and join the dance." – Alan Watts

I used to think uncertainty was the enemy. Like most people, I craved predictability - a clear path forward, reliable outcomes, and the comfortable illusion that I could control what happened next. Then life, with its characteristic blend of wisdom and mischief, taught me otherwise. Through a series of unexpected plot twists that would have made a soap opera writer proud, I learned that uncertainty isn't the opposite of security - it's actually the birthplace of possibility.

We're living through what some visionary teachers call the "chaotic nodes" - those pivotal moments when everything familiar seems to be shifting at once. The old rules aren't working, the maps don't match the territory anymore, and honestly, sometimes it feels like we're all just making it up as we go along. Which, it turns out, might be exactly what we need to do.

Acknowledging the Darkness Without Turning Away

Here's something I learned the hard way: what you resist, persists. For years, whenever life got messy or uncertain, my instinct was to look away, distract myself, or wait for things to "get back to normal." But here's the thing about our current moment - there might not be a "normal" to get back to. We're in uncharted waters, and the sooner we accept that, the sooner we can learn to navigate them skillfully.

Right now, we're witnessing what feels like a convergence of everything challenging: climate disruption, economic instability, political upheaval, social fragmentation, and technological changes that are reshaping human consciousness faster than we can adapt. These aren't separate crises but symptoms of a deeper transition - what some call the shift from an industrial growth society to something we haven't fully imagined yet.

The first step in navigating uncertainty isn't positive thinking or premature optimism. It's what I call "clear seeing" - the willingness to look directly at what's actually happening without the comforting filters of denial or wishful thinking. This takes courage, but it's the kind of mature courage that says, "I can handle the truth, even when it's uncomfortable."

When we stop turning away from difficulty, something remarkable happens. We discover that we're more resilient than we thought, more creative than we imagined, and more connected to sources of wisdom and strength than we previously realized. The very act of facing reality without flinching begins to transform both us and our circumstances.

The Era of Multiple Realities

If you've been feeling like you're living in a different universe from some of your neighbors, friends, or family members, you're not alone. We've entered what some call the "post-truth era," though I think it's more accurate to say we're living through a time of "multiple realities."

Where previous generations might have disagreed about policies or interpretations, we now seem to inhabit entirely different versions of what's actually happening. This isn't just about political spin - it's about the fundamental challenge of navigating a world where competing narratives about reality coexist in the same cultural space.

This multiplicity emerges from several factors: information technology has democratized storytelling, allowing anyone to broadcast their version of truth. Algorithms create information bubbles that reinforce existing beliefs while filtering out contradictory evidence. The pace of change has accelerated beyond our ability to process, leaving us vulnerable to simplistic explanations that promise to make sense of overwhelming complexity.

Meanwhile, advances in quantum physics and consciousness research are revealing that reality itself might be more fluid and observer-dependent than our mechanistic worldview assumed. Perhaps this isn't a problem to be solved but a condition to be navigated with wisdom and skill.

Learning to navigate multiple realities requires developing what I think of as "cognitive flexibility" - the ability to shift between different ways of seeing as the situation requires, while staying connected to deeper truths that transcend any particular perspective.

The Three C's: Courage, Curiosity, and Creativity

When the old rules no longer apply and new ones haven't emerged yet, three qualities become essential: Courage, Curiosity, and Creativity. These aren't just nice-to-have virtues - they're practical necessities for anyone who wants to thrive during times of transition.

Courage isn't the absence of fear but the willingness to act constructively even when afraid or uncertain. In our context, this means facing difficult truths about our collective situation, questioning assumptions that no longer serve, trying new approaches without guarantees, and staying open-hearted despite unprecedented challenges. It's the quiet courage of showing up fully to whatever each day brings.

Curiosity serves as an antidote to our mind's natural tendency to reach for simple explanations and premature conclusions. When faced with complexity, genuine curiosity keeps us open to new information, unexpected possibilities, and surprising solutions. Instead of asking "Why me?" when difficulties arise, curious people ask "What might this teach me?" and "How can I grow through this experience?"

Creativity becomes essential when old solutions no longer work and new ones haven't yet emerged. This isn't just artistic expression but the broader capacity to generate novel responses to novel situations. It's learning to see chaos not as the enemy of order but as the fertile ground from which new forms of order emerge.

Here's a concrete example that brings this concept to life:

Your company announces a major restructuring, eliminating your entire department. The old playbook—polish your resume, network within your industry, apply to similar roles—yields nothing but dead ends for months. The job market has shifted, your skills feel obsolete, and the chaos of uncertainty is overwhelming. Instead of fighting harder to recreate what you had, you sit with the discomfort. You start noticing what energizes you in the mess: those side conversations you've been having about sustainable packaging, the way you've been helping friends troubleshoot their small business logistics. You begin combining your operations background with this emerging interest in completely unexpected ways. You reach out to local eco-friendly startups—not with a polished pitch, but with genuine curiosity and half-formed ideas about supply chain problems you've noticed. One conversation leads to another. Three months later, you're consulting for four small businesses, stitching together income streams you never would have planned for. It's messy and non-linear, nothing like the clear career path you had, but it's working—and it only emerged because you stopped trying to force the old order back into existence.

When Old Maps No Longer Match the Territory

One of the most disorienting aspects of transitional times is discovering that the mental maps we inherited don't match the territory we're trying to navigate. The assumptions about how careers work, what constitutes security, how to plan for the future - all these inherited frameworks may need updating for current conditions.

The old model of expertise assumed specialists could master discrete domains and provide authoritative guidance. But in a world of accelerating change and increasing interconnection, expertise itself becomes provisional. The career planning model of "choose, develop, climb" breaks down when entire industries transform overnight. The financial security model of "work, save, invest" becomes questionable when economic systems themselves are in flux.

This doesn't mean abandoning all wisdom from the past but learning to distinguish between timeless principles that remain relevant and time-bound strategies that may no longer serve. The underlying human needs for safety, belonging, purpose, and meaning remain constant, but how we meet these needs must be continuously adapted.

I think of maps and territories often these days. All mental models are simplifications of reality - useful when they help us navigate effectively, dangerous when we mistake them for reality itself. In times of rapid change, the ability to hold our maps lightly, and navigate without them when necessary, becomes crucial.

The Polynesian Art of Wayfinding

Perhaps no tradition offers more relevant wisdom for our current moment than the ancient Polynesian practice of wayfinding - the art of ocean navigation without instruments. For thousands of years, Polynesian navigators used this skill to discover and settle islands across the vast Pacific Ocean, a feat that still amazes modern sailors.

Traditional wayfinders, like Moana in the Disney film, underwent years of training to read subtle signs that could guide them across thousands of miles of open ocean. They navigated by stars, using celestial bodies to maintain direction and estimate position. They studied wave patterns, feeling how swells reflected off distant islands. They observed bird flight patterns, water color, cloud formations - countless natural phenomena that provided navigation information.

Most remarkably, these navigators found tiny islands in the vast Pacific not by following predetermined routes but by reading the dynamic, ever-changing conditions of the ocean itself. They understood that successful navigation required flexible response to constantly changing conditions rather than rigid adherence to fixed plans.

The wayfinding tradition offers crucial lessons: **Trust your inner compass** - develop your ability to sense what's true and beneficial even when you can't prove it rationally. **Read the signs** - learn to recognize patterns and signals about emerging trends and opportunities. **Navigate by principles, not plans** - use consistent values like compassion and integrity to guide you when rigid plans become obsolete. **Embrace the journey** - find meaning in the process of positive change rather than waiting for some future state of resolution.

Entering the Doldrums

Every ocean navigator knows about the doldrums - equatorial regions where trade winds die away, leaving ships motionless in eerily still waters. For traditional vessels, this meant potential disaster without wind to power their journey.

We're currently in a collective version of the doldrums. Many external systems that previously provided guidance - political institutions, economic structures, educational systems - are themselves in crisis. The familiar landmarks have disappeared into fog.

But experienced navigators learned to use the doldrums differently. When external forces became unavailable, they relied more completely on inner resources - celestial navigation, subtle current patterns, and trust in deeper rhythms that weren't immediately visible.

When we can't depend on external authorities, we must learn to navigate by principles that transcend current circumstances: timeless values like compassion and justice, the evolutionary impulse toward greater consciousness, and our ability to distinguish between what serves life and what destroys it.

Cultivating Transitional Intelligence

Navigating uncertainty requires developing what I call "transitional intelligence" - the capacity to sense emerging possibilities even when they're not yet visible, maintain hope when current conditions seem hopeless, and take constructive action without seeing the whole path ahead.

This includes several key capacities: **Flexibility of timing**- the ability to shift between different time scales, zooming out to see long-term patterns while addressing immediate needs. **Sustaining paradox** - holding apparent contradictions without immediately resolving them, being simultaneously hopeful and realistic, engaged and detached. **Awareness of things emerging**- sensing new possibilities trying to emerge from current conditions, like recognizing the forest that wants to grow from what looks like cleared land.

These abilities can be developed through meditation that opens access to deeper knowing, engaging with complexity rather than seeking premature closure, cultivating relationships with diverse perspectives, spending time in nature to attune to larger rhythms, and practicing what systems thinkers call "sensing" - learning to feel into emerging future possibilities.

The Human Tendency to Create the Future from the Past

One of the greatest obstacles to navigating uncertainty skillfully is our tendency to project the future based on patterns from the past. This made sense when changes happened slowly, but in times of rapid transformation, it becomes problematic.

When we unconsciously assume the future will resemble the past, we miss opportunities to participate consciously in creating genuinely new possibilities. We get trapped in "solutions of yesterday" rather than developing "solutions of tomorrow."

This manifests everywhere: individuals responding to new challenges with old psychological strategies, organizations trying to solve current problems with outdated structures, societies addressing contemporary challenges with institutions designed for previous eras.

Breaking free requires developing **"future memory"** - the capacity to sense not just what was but what wants to emerge. Indigenous traditions speak of making decisions based on their impact seven generations into the future. This long-term perspective helps break the tyranny of immediate reactions and inherited patterns.

A New Age of Discovery

Rather than seeing uncertainty as a problem to overcome, we might reframe it as an invitation to participate in what could be called a "New Age of Discovery" - not conquest and colonization, but conscious exploration of human potential and planetary possibility.

Just as Polynesian navigators ventured into the vast Pacific without knowing what they'd find but trusting their ability to navigate whatever they encountered, we're called to explore uncharted territories of consciousness, relationship, and social organization.

This New Age of Discovery is both external and internal. Externally, we're exploring new forms of energy, communication, and social organization that could enable sustainable prosperity. Internally, we're discovering new capacities of human consciousness - abilities to access information and wisdom in ways our ancestors never imagined.

This reframing transforms uncertainty from something to be feared into something to be explored. Instead of seeing ourselves as victims of forces beyond our control, we become pioneering explorers of new territories of possibility.

The Navigation Continues

The art of navigating uncertainty isn't something we master once and possess forever. Like the ocean itself, uncertainty is dynamic and ever-changing, requiring continuous attention and adaptation. Each challenge we successfully navigate builds capacity for the next one.

Perhaps most importantly, we're not navigating alone. Like Polynesian navigators who shared knowledge and supported each other's journeys, we're part of a vast community learning to find our way in uncharted territories. Our individual navigation skills serve not only our own journey but the collective human voyage toward whatever new lands of possibility await discovery.

The flame we nurture through these challenging times isn't just our own but part of a larger light illuminating the path for all travelers. In learning to navigate uncertainty with skill and wisdom, we contribute to the great work of our time: transforming crisis into opportunity, chaos into creativity, and uncertainty into wonder. The strength you build getting through your own hard times doesn't just stay with you. When your friend calls, panicking about their own upheaval, you'll find yourself saying something real and useful—not platitudes, but actual insight born from your own stumbling. Your teenage daughter will watch how you handle not having all the answers, and years later, she'll remember that when she faces her own crossroads.

What we're all doing right now—learning to function when the ground keeps shifting, finding our footing in the unfamiliar—

this matters beyond our individual lives. Every time you choose curiosity over panic, every time you experiment instead of freezing, you're mapping terrain that others will walk too. You're proving it's possible to not just survive uncertainty, but to let it crack you open to possibilities you'd never considered when everything felt solid and predictable.

Your particular struggles, your specific breakthroughs—they become part of the lived wisdom we're all building together about how to be human in times that don't come with instructions

The ocean is vast, the journey is long, and the destination isn't yet visible. But we have stars to guide us, currents to carry us, and the accumulated wisdom of countless generations who faced their own uncertainties with courage and skill. Most importantly, we have each other = fellow wayfarers sharing the great adventure of conscious evolution.

The art of navigating uncertainty isn't about eliminating the unknown but learning to dance with it. In embracing this art, we discover that uncertainty might be one of our greatest teachers - the condition that calls forth our deepest wisdom, greatest creativity, and most profound capacity for love in action.

The flame burns bright in the darkness. The navigation continues. The new world awaits.

Reflective Prompts: - What certainties am I clinging to that no longer serve? - Where in my life am I being invited to become a wayfinder? - How might I cultivate courage, curiosity, and creativity this week?

Practice: - Each evening, spend five minutes in silence and ask: *What did I notice today that wasn't part of any map I've*

known? What unknown parts of me are trying to emerge? What signals am I getting in my life that confirm this? Keep a log of emerging signs, symbols, and intuitions. What situations and events trigger fear and anxiety in me?

Mantra: *The unknown is my friend.*

Further Reading:

David la Chapelle: *Navigating the Tides of Change*

Reshad Feild: *The Last Barrier*

James Ogilvy: *Living without a Goal*

Llewelyn Vaughn-Lee: *Darkening of the Light*

Chapter 2: The Art of Critical Thinking

Discernment in the Digital Age

"Follow your heart. But take your brain with you." - Alfred Adler

"I will not let anyone walk through my mind with their dirty feet."
- Mahatma Gandhi

Let me tell you something that might make you uncomfortable: your mind is under siege. Right now, as you're reading this, there's a battle raging for control of your most precious real estate—the space between your ears. And frankly, you might be losing.

I don't say this to scare you (well, maybe a little), but to wake you up to something our ancestors understood instinctively: the quality of our thinking determines the quality of our lives. They called it discernment, or sometimes "discernment of spirits" - the sacred art of telling truth from lies, wisdom from manipulation, and authentic insight from clever packaging.

Today, we desperately need to resurrect this ancient skill, because the battle for your mind has never been more sophisticated or relentless.

Welcome to the Mental Wild West

Picture the American frontier of the early 1800s—vast, untamed territories that everyone wanted to claim. Now imagine that frontier is your consciousness, and instead of gold prospectors and cattle ranchers, you've got corporate marketers, political operatives, social media algorithms, and various other digital desperados all trying to stake their claim on your mental landscape.

The difference is, you probably knew when someone was trying to steal your physical land. Mental colonization is sneakier. It happens while you're scrolling through your phone, binge-watching Netflix, or just trying to catch up on the news. Before you know it, your thoughts aren't entirely your own anymore—they're a curious mix of advertising jingles, political talking points, and whatever the algorithm thinks will keep you engaged (which usually means outraged).

I realized this was happening to me a few years ago when I caught myself humming a commercial jingle while making coffee. Not just any jingle—one for a product I didn't even use, from a company I didn't particularly like. Somehow, their little earworm had taken up residence in my brain without paying rent. That's when it hit me: if they could colonize my morning coffee routine, what else had they claimed?

The Great Information Flood

We like to call this the "information age," but that's like calling a tsunami a "water event." What we're actually experiencing is an unprecedented deluge of data, opinions, facts, lies, theories, and hot takes, all mixed together in a swirling torrent that makes it nearly impossible to distinguish between what's nourishing and what's toxic.

Everything that reaches you has already been filtered—by algorithms that know your psychological profile better than you do, by editors with their own agendas, by corporations trying to sell you something, and by your own unconscious biases that were programmed into you before you were old enough to question them.

It's like trying to drink from a fire hose while wearing someone else's glasses. No wonder we're all a bit dizzy.

The Pandemics Nobody Talks About

While everyone was focused on COVID-19 (understandably), two other pandemics were spreading even faster: the fear pandemic and the spiritual emptiness pandemic. And unlike the virus, these don't require physical proximity to spread—they transmit through Wi-Fi.

The fear pandemic is obvious once you notice it. We're living in a constant state of low-level anxiety about everything: economic collapse, climate change, political chaos, social rejection, health crises, and whatever new catastrophe happened to trend on social media today. Our nervous systems, designed for handling immediate physical threats, are now on permanent high alert for dangers that may never materialize.

Meanwhile, the spiritual pandemic has left millions feeling empty despite material abundance. When the primary cultural message is that consciousness is just brain chemistry, love is just evolutionary programming, and meaning is just a story we tell ourselves, is it any wonder that depression rates are skyrocketing?

The cure for both pandemics starts revisiting your relationship with mass media and reclaiming the sovereignty of your own mind.

The Socratic Solution

About 2,400 years ago, the man that we now consider the Father of Philosophy, Socrates, wandered around Athens badgering its citizens with questions. He had the habit of approaching people who thought they were experts and asking them to explain what they claimed to know. Pretty soon, through careful questioning, he'd reveal that they didn't really understand their subject as well as they thought.

This wasn't intellectual bullying—it was intellectual midwifery. Socrates believed that wisdom was already within people; his job was just to help them give birth to it through the right questions. His students learned not by being told what to think, but by being taught how to think.

The Socratic method works something like this: instead of accepting statements at face value, you keep asking "Why?" and "How do you know that?" A student might claim, "Justice is giving everyone what they deserve." Socrates would respond, "Interesting. But what does it mean to 'deserve' something? And who decides what someone deserves?" Pretty soon, what seemed like a simple concept reveals layers of complexity that demand deeper thought.

His most famous insight was admitting "I know that I don't know" - not because he was ignorant, but because he recognized that true wisdom begins with intellectual humility. The people who thought they already had all the answers were the ones most resistant to learning anything new.

The Socratic method—asking probing questions rather than accepting surface answers—is more relevant today than ever. Instead of swallowing information whole, we can learn to ask: "How do I know this is true? What evidence supports this claim? Who benefits if I believe this? What am I not being told?"

These questions are like intellectual immune system boosters. They help you develop resistance to mental viruses that would otherwise colonize your consciousness without your permission.

The Buddhist Witness

Here's something I learned from meditation that changed everything: you are not your thoughts. You're the awareness that notices your thoughts. This might sound obvious, but most of us live completely identified with whatever is churning through our mental machinery.

The Buddhists call this the "witness consciousness"- the part of you that can step back and observe your mental and emotional processes without being swept away by them. It's like being a meteorologist instead of someone caught in the storm. You can see the weather patterns without letting them determine your mood.

I practice this while reading news or scrolling social media. Instead of immediately reacting to whatever information I encounter, I pause and notice: "Ah, anger is arising. Interesting. What about this triggered that response? What might I be missing? What would I need to know to have a more complete understanding?"

This simple shift from identification to observation creates space for actual thinking instead of just reacting.

Your Body's Built-In Lie Detector

Here's something they don't teach in school: your body is smarter than your brain when it comes to detecting deception. While your mind can be fooled by clever arguments and emotional manipulation, your nervous system often knows immediately when something is off.

Pay attention to how different types of information affect you physically. Does reading this news article make your stomach tighten? Does listening to this person speak make you feel energized or drained? Does this idea make you want to lean forward with interest or lean back with suspicion?

Your body is constantly processing information that your conscious mind misses—micro-expressions, energy patterns, inconsistencies between words and tone. Learning to read these somatic signals is like having a built-in BS detector. And a very reliable one at that. Often I have second guessed my body's reaction to something or someone, only to realize later that my gut response was accurate.

Of course, your body can also be influenced by your conditioning and fears, so don't make it the final authority. But do include its wisdom in your decision-making process.

The Fundamentals of Clear Thinking

Now for some practical tools to sharpen your discernment. Think of these as your mental self-defense kit:

Beware of Confirmation Bias: We all have a tendency to seek out information that confirms what we already believe while ignoring evidence that challenges us. It feels good to be right, but it's terrible for learning. Actively seek out perspectives that make you uncomfortable. Your beliefs should be strong enough to survive some questioning—if they're not, maybe they need upgrading.

I once had a friend who only read news sources that aligned with his political views. When I asked why, he said, "I don't want to pollute my mind with lies." But here's the thing: if your worldview can't handle exposure to different perspectives, it might not be as solid as you think. Strong ideas get stronger when challenged; weak ideas crumble. Better to discover the weak spots now than have reality expose them later. Remember Socrates!

Embrace the Grey Zone: Carl Jung noted that life rarely offers black-and-white choices—most of reality exists in various shades of grey. Anyone offering simple solutions to complex problems is probably selling something. Real wisdom usually involves holding multiple perspectives simultaneously and being comfortable with ambiguity as well as paradox.

This is particularly challenging in our polarized culture, where nuance is treated as weakness and certainty as strength. But the most interesting conversations I've had are with people who can say things like, "I generally support this point of view, but I understand the legitimate concerns on the other side", or "This situation is more complicated than either side is willing to admit."

Question Simple Solutions: When someone promises that complex problems have easy fixes, reach for your skeptical hat. Climate change, economic inequality, political dysfunction, personal relationships - these challenges exist precisely because they don't have simple solutions. If the answers were obvious, we would have implemented them already.

This doesn't mean giving up on solutions, but it does mean being wary of anyone who promises that voting for the right candidate, buying the right product, or following the right guru will solve all your problems.

Check Your Sources: Always ask who's telling you something and what they might gain from your believing it. Is this person qualified to speak on this topic? Do they have financial, political, or ideological motivations? Are they citing credible sources or just repeating what someone else said?

I learned this lesson the hard way when I shared what seemed like an important health article on to friends, only to discover later that it was funded by a company selling the exact supplements the article recommended. Now I always ask: who paid for this research? Who benefits from these conclusions?

Practice Intellectual Humility: The smartest people I know are comfortable saying "I don't know" and "I might be wrong." Certainty is overrated - curiosity is where the real learning happens. When someone acts like they have all the answers, I get suspicious. The universe is vast and mysterious; anyone who claims to have it all figured out probably hasn't been paying attention.

Engage Ideas, Not Just Personalities: It's easier to dismiss ideas by attacking the people who hold them than to engage with the ideas themselves. But this intellectual laziness prevents us from learning. Try this experiment: find someone you disagree with and see if you can identify at least one point they make that has merit, regardless of how you feel about them personally.

Maintain Wonder: Cynicism masquerades as sophistication, but it's actually a form of intellectual and spiritual laziness. The cynical person has decided that everything is corrupt, meaningless, disappointing, manipulative or doomed, which conveniently eliminates the need to evaluate each situation on its merits, accept the good with the bad or even occasionally be disappointed. Nothing ventured, nothing lost. Stay curious about the world. Avoid cynics, they drain the life out of you. There's always more to discover, more to understand, more to marvel at. Life is an adventure, if you want it to be.

I've noticed that the most cynical people are often those who used to be extremely naive. When their innocent worldview got shattered, they swung to the opposite extreme. But wisdom lies in the middle—being neither gullible nor cynical, but discerning.

Italian Wisdom

There is a wonderful Italian proverb that goes: "If you don't use your brain, you might as well fry it!" (brain actually is a delicacy in parts of Italy). This captures something essential. Mental muscles, like physical ones, atrophy without exercise. If you let algorithms do your thinking, advertisers shape your desires, and pundits form your opinions, don't be surprised when your capacity for independent thought starts to feel a bit rusty.

Use it or lose it, as they say. Engage with challenging ideas. Read books that make you think. Have conversations with people who disagree with you. Question your assumptions regularly. Treat your mind like the precious resource it is.

Taking Back Your Territory

Here's the bottom line: in a world where everyone wants a piece of your mind, maintaining mental sovereignty isn't just a nice idea - it's an act of survival. Every thought you think, every belief you hold, every decision you make ripples out into the world and affects not just your life but the lives of everyone around you.

When you learn to think clearly, question skillfully, and discern wisely, you're not just protecting yourself from manipulation - you're contributing to the collective intelligence of our species. We desperately need people who can see through propaganda, resist fearmongering, and think beyond tribal loyalties.

The ancient art of discernment isn't about becoming paranoid or cynical. It's about becoming awake. It's about reclaiming your birthright as a conscious being capable of independent thought and wise action.

Your mind is your most precious territory. Guard it well, use it wisely, and remember—in the battle for human consciousness, every awakened mind makes a difference.

The frontier is still wild, but now you're armed with the tools to navigate it skillfully. Use them well.

Reflection Prompts: - What are the primary sources shaping my worldview right now? - When was the last time I changed my mind, and why? - What values do I use to filter information? - How do I respond when someone challenges my perspective? When was the last time I listened to my body's reaction to a truth or fallacy, and did I honor it?

Practice: - Try a "news fast" for three days. Instead, observe your inner landscape. Engage with one belief or idea you disagree with. Try to articulate its value without judgment. - Find a friend and debate a topic from the opposite side without taking it personally. - Create a media diet: how much and what do you consume, and what effect does it have on you?

Mantra: *I am the master of my mind: I am the captain of my ship.* (inspired by the poem *Invictus* by William Ernest Henley)

Further Reading:

Daniel Kahneman: *Thinking, Fast and Slow*

Hans Rosling: *Factfulness*

David A. Levy: *Tools of Critical Thinking*

Neil deGrasse Tyson: *Starry Messenger: Cosmic Perspectives on Civilization*

Yuval Noah Harari: *Sapiens*

Chapter 3: Resilience

The Art of Bending Without Breaking

"The bamboo that bends is stronger than the oak that resists." - Japanese Proverb

"You have power over your mind, not outside events. Realize this, and you will find strength." – Marcus Aurelius

If I've learned anything from my years on this planet, it's that life has a peculiar sense of humor. Just when you think you've got everything figured out, life shows up with a curveball, a plot twist, or what I like to call a "cosmic oh heck moment." The question isn't whether these moments will come - they will. The question is whether you'll meet them with the flexibility of bamboo or the rigidity of an old oak tree.

Resilience isn't about being tough as nails or developing an emotional shell so thick that nothing can penetrate it. That's not resilience - that's just armor, and armor is heavy. True resilience is more like learning to dance with uncertainty, to find your footing on shifting ground, and to discover that you're far more bendable than you ever imagined.

The Chinese Wisdom of Crisis

In the Chinese language, the word for "crisis" (危机) is composed of two ideograms: *wei* (危), meaning **danger**, and *ji* (

机), meaning **opportunity**. This etymology, while sometimes debated linguistically, is deeply **symbolic** and spiritually resonant. Every crisis carries within it a dual potential: the threat of breakdown and the seed of breakthrough.

We often resist this idea. Pain, loss, failure, and hardship can feel like signs that something has gone terribly wrong. But what if life is not meant to be smooth, predictable, or easy? What if life is a school?

The ancient Stoics saw life this way. So did the early Christian mystics. So do many Eastern paths. To live, truly live, is to be **apprenticed to the soul**. And the soul does not learn only through pleasure and success -it is shaped most profoundly through pressure and difficulty. The soul yearns for experience, and that experience comes both in delightful and unpleasant packages.

Life's Curriculum

I've come to believe that life operates like a very creative—and sometimes mischievous—university. The curriculum includes subjects we'd prefer not to take, professors we'd rather avoid, and exams we feel unprepared for. But here's the thing: we don't get to skip the required courses.

Some classes are gentle introductions—minor disappointments that teach us about resilience in manageable doses. Others are advanced seminars that challenge everything we thought we knew about ourselves. The difficult relationships that push our buttons, the career setbacks that humble our egos, the losses that break our hearts open - these aren't accidents or punishments. They're part of the curriculum.

There is a popular expression "I am not what happened to me, I am what I choose to become." Our experiences don't define us - our responses to them do. This is simultaneously terrifying and liberating. Terrifying because it means we can't blame our circumstances for our happiness. Liberating because it means we're not victims of those circumstances either.

The key insight is that growth often requires discomfort. Just as physical muscles need resistance to grow stronger, psychological resilience develops through encountering and working through challenges. This doesn't mean seeking out suffering—life provides plenty without our help—but it does mean reframing difficulties as opportunities for development rather than evidence that something has gone wrong.

The Modern Myth of Entitled Ease

Let's talk about one of our culture's most damaging beliefs: the idea that life should be easy, that we deserve constant happiness, and that discomfort indicates failure. This myth is relatively new in human history, and it's making us psychologically fragile in ways our ancestors would find puzzling.

Previous generations expected life to be challenging. They understood that comfort was temporary, that loss was inevitable, and that character was built through enduring difficulties rather than avoiding them. They didn't have self-help gurus promising them their "best life now" or social media feeds showcasing everyone else's highlight reels.

This entitled attitude toward ease creates what I call "psychological thin skin" - a condition where normal life challenges feel overwhelming because we've been led to believe they shouldn't exist. When difficulties arise, instead of thinking "This is life being life," we think "This is wrong, this shouldn't be happening to me."

I see this frequently in the young people I encounter. They live in a world where discomfort can often be eliminated with the click of a button—too hot? Adjust the thermostat. Bored? Check your phone. Hungry? Order delivery. While these conveniences aren't inherently bad, they can create an expectation that all discomfort should be immediately solvable.

The antidote isn't to seek out suffering but to develop a more realistic - and ultimately more hopeful - understanding of human existence. Life includes both joy and sorrow, success and failure, comfort and challenge. The difficult parts aren't bugs in the system; they're features.

Many New Age teachings today suggest that suffering or scarcity reflect some failure on our part—as though we could buy, practice, or strive our way into guaranteed abundance. The promise is often implicit: do more, and you will be rewarded with material, emotional, and physical well-being. Meister Eckhart, the medieval German mystic, cautioned against this "merchant attitude" toward the Divine, a spirit of exchange that says, *I will do this, if You give me that.* Yet the soul's path is rarely so transactional. We cannot fully know which wounds we are meant to heal or what experiences our soul has chosen for its growth. Healing and grace are always possible, but they cannot be measured in material terms. Abundance comes in many forms— sometimes visible, sometimes hidden—and it often reveals itself in ways far deeper than wealth or success.

The Biology of Adaptation

From a biological standpoint, resilience is mirrored in the most intelligent and persistent life forms on Earth: **viruses**. These tiny packets of genetic material have no brains, no nervous systems, no sentience—and yet they are masters of adaptation. They can mutate rapidly to changing environments. They find new ways to survive.

We are more than viruses. We are conscious beings with choice, imagination, and purpose. But **we must learn from nature**. Life is change. To resist change is to suffer. To adapt consciously is to grow.

This principle of biological resilience also reveals that challenge itself often strengthens systems. Muscles grow stronger under resistance. Immune systems develop robustness when exposed to manageable threats. Psychological resilience increases when we successfully navigate difficulties. The principle of hormesis—where small doses of stress actually benefit organisms—applies as much to emotional development as physical conditioning.

Charles Darwin is often misquoted as saying only the strongest survive. In truth, his insight was subtler: *those who survive are those most responsive to change.*

Resilience, then, is not strength in the rigid sense. It is the **agility of the body, mind and soul**.

But here's what's interesting: agility and adaptation doesn't mean abandoning your core identity. Water remains water whether it's in a glass or a river. Trees remain trees whether they're standing straight or bending in wind. Similarly, we can adapt our responses to circumstances while maintaining our essential values and character.

The Stockdale Paradox

Admiral James Stockdale spent over seven years as a prisoner of war in Vietnam, including four years in solitary confinement. His observations about survival under extreme conditions offer profound insights into the psychology of resilience.

The paradox that bears his name emerged from his study of which prisoners were most likely to survive. Surprisingly, it wasn't the eternal optimists who constantly predicted imminent release. When their predictions repeatedly failed, these prisoners often fell into despair. Nor was it the pessimists who assumed they'd never get out—they sometimes lost the motivation necessary for survival.

The survivors were those who could simultaneously hold two seemingly contradictory perspectives: unwavering faith that they would ultimately prevail, combined with the discipline to confront the brutal facts of their current reality without false hope.

This paradox applies far beyond prison camps. Whether you're dealing with a serious illness, a difficult relationship, financial struggles, or career setbacks, the key is maintaining long-term faith while addressing short-term realities honestly. It's the difference between wishful thinking (which ignores current challenges) and mature hope (which acknowledges them while maintaining trust in eventual positive outcomes).

I think of an ex-colleague Tom, who was diagnosed with a serious illness. Instead of either pretending everything was fine or surrendering to despair, he said, "I'm going to beat this thing, but first I need to understand exactly what I'm dealing with." He researched his condition thoroughly, followed his treatment plan religiously, and made practical arrangements for his family—all while maintaining absolute certainty that he would recover. That's the Stockdale Paradox in action.

The Psychology of Self-Actualization

Abraham Maslow's research into self-actualizing individuals—those rare people who seem to realize their full potential—reveals crucial insights about resilience. These individuals share characteristics that enable them not just to survive challenges but to use them as stepping stones to extraordinary growth.

Self-actualizing people see reality clearly rather than through the lens of wishful thinking or defensive denial. They accept themselves and others without wasting energy fighting unchangeable aspects of reality. They respond spontaneously to situations rather than following rigid scripts. They focus on solving problems rather than dwelling on how problems affect them personally.

Perhaps most importantly, they maintain what Maslow called a "philosophical sense of humor"—the ability to find genuine lightness even in difficult situations, not as denial but as perspective. They can laugh at life's absurdities, including their own, without becoming cynical or cruel.

These aren't innate gifts but developed capacities. They represent the fruit of choosing growth over comfort, meaning over ease, and service over self-protection consistently over time. The good news is that anyone can cultivate these qualities, though it requires patience and practice.

Three Pillars of Resilient Response

Research has identified core strategies that characterize people who not only survive adversity but emerge stronger. Understanding these can significantly enhance our capacity to navigate challenges.

First Pillar: Accepting Suffering as Normal

The Buddhist First Noble Truth states that life contains *dukkha*—suffering or dissatisfaction that comes from the impermanent nature of existence. This isn't pessimistic but realistic. When we understand that difficulties are normal rather than aberrant, we're less likely to add psychological suffering to inevitable physical or emotional pain.

Resilient people don't ask "Why me?" when challenges arise because they understand that difficulties visit everyone. They don't interpret setbacks as personal failures or cosmic unfairness but as confirmation of their membership in the human community. This prevents the victim mentality that amplifies suffering and interferes with effective response.

Instead, they ask empowering questions: "What can I learn from this? How might this serve my growth? What strengths might I discover? How can this experience help me serve others facing similar challenges?"

Second Pillar: Focusing on Positive Outcomes

While accepting present difficulties, resilient people maintain focus on positive possibilities. This isn't denial but strategic attention management—choosing to water seeds of possibility rather than weeds of desperation.

This manifests in several ways: drawing strength from spiritual practices that provide meaning beyond immediate circumstances, actively seeking support from others, approaching difficulties as puzzles to solve rather than punishments to endure, focusing on small achievable steps rather than overwhelming big pictures, and actively looking for ways their challenges might serve larger purposes.

The Serenity Prayer captures this beautifully: "Grant me the serenity to accept the things I cannot change, courage to change the things I can, and wisdom to know the difference." It's about maintaining agency where possible while accepting what's beyond our control.

Third Pillar: Building Anti-Fragility

Beyond surviving challenges or bouncing back, the most resilient people develop what researcher Nassim Taleb calls "anti-fragility"—the capacity to grow stronger through stress.

Like bones that become denser under weight-bearing exercise, they use difficulties as opportunities to develop new capabilities.

This involves reframing adversity as training, building diverse sources of meaning and identity, developing emotional regulation skills, creating systems for learning from experience, practicing gratitude even during difficulties, maintaining physical health to support psychological resilience, and finding ways to serve others facing similar challenges.

Perhaps most importantly, anti-fragile people understand that their struggles can become sources of strength for others. This transforms suffering from meaningless pain into meaningful contribution, creating what psychologists call "post-traumatic growth."

The Long View

One of the most powerful tools for resilience is what we might call "the Long View"—the ability to see current circumstances within larger contexts of meaning and purpose. This doesn't require religious belief but involves cultivating the capacity to zoom out from immediate difficulties to see bigger pictures. Literature is full of great tales of the Journey of the Hero that focus on the quality of resilience. One of the great classics of all times, Homer's *Ulysses* is timeless tale of a protagonist facing all manner of trials, in the form of betrayals, enemies, monsters, vengeful gods and goddesses to name but a few; in the end he prevails and may return home, strengthened and transformed.

This journey is not reserved for epic heroes. It is **our journey**.

When we lose a job, fall ill, experience heartbreak, or face existential doubt, we are being initiated. We are being asked to descend into the unknown. The resilient person does not avoid this descent - they move through it with courage and eventually return with wisdom to offer the world.

From this expanded viewpoint, many daily dramas reveal themselves as temporary fluctuations in larger stories of growth and contribution. The career setback that feels catastrophic today may become the catalyst for discovering a more authentic path. The relationship that ends painfully may clear space for deeper connections.

Einstein famously said:" "There are only two ways to live your life. One is as though nothing is a miracle. The other is as though everything is a miracle." It's the choice between seeing the universe as friendly or unfriendly, and it is one of the most important decisions we make. This choice doesn't depend on external circumstances but on our fundamental orientation toward existence. Choosing to see life as fundamentally supportive of our growth creates the psychological foundation for resilience.

The Paradox of Our Times

We live in an era requiring unprecedented resilience while simultaneously creating conditions that undermine its development. We have access to more resources than any previous generation, yet we're often more psychologically fragile. We have more choices and opportunities, yet higher rates of anxiety and depression.

An example of this paradox is Sarah. She is 28, has a master's degree, works remotely for a tech company making $85,000 a year, can access therapy via an app on her phone, has a meditation subscription, a fitness tracker, and can Google any question instantly. Her grandmother at the same age was raising four kids in a two-bedroom house on a factory worker's salary, with no degree and few choices about her life path.

Yet Sarah lies awake at 2 AM paralyzed by career decisions. Should she stay in tech or pursue her passion for environmental work? Take the promotion or preserve work-life balance?

Move to Austin, Barcelona, or stay put? She's compared her salary to industry benchmarks, analyzed her personality type, listened to seven podcasts about finding purpose, and still feels stuck. Her therapist costs $80 per session even with insurance. She's on her second antidepressant. Her Apple Watch keeps reminding her to breathe.

Her grandmother, who had far fewer options, somehow had a steadier internal compass. Not because life was easier—it was objectively harder—but because the abundance of choice itself, the constant comparison with curated lives on Instagram, the pressure to optimize everything, the erosion of any default path... these create a different kind of suffering.

Sarah has resources her grandmother couldn't imagine. But she also carries psychological burdens her grandmother never faced. More tools for thriving; less capacity to use them.

This paradox creates both challenge and opportunity. The same technologies that can overwhelm us also provide access to wisdom, support communities, and resources for growth. The same global awareness that can create anxiety also opens us to inspiration from examples of resilience worldwide.

The key is learning to navigate this complexity wisely - using technology as a tool for connection rather than escape, embracing global awareness without becoming paralyzed by problems we can't directly solve, and drawing inspiration from others while focusing on our own growth and contribution.

The Gift Hidden in Plain Sight

Ultimately, resilience reveals adversity as one of life's unexpected gifts. Not because suffering is inherently good, but because our responses to difficulty can generate qualities of character and depths of compassion that might never emerge through ease alone.

Every person who has developed genuine wisdom has traveled through valleys of challenge. Every great contribution to human wellbeing has emerged from someone's willingness to transform their struggles into service. Every breakthrough in human understanding has come from someone's refusal to be defeated by apparent failure.

One of the shining examples of resilience is the life of Nelson Mandela. Nelson Mandela spent 27 years in prison—breaking rocks in a limestone quarry on Robben Island, sleeping on a thin mat on a concrete floor, allowed one visitor per year. He was 44 when he entered prison, 71 when he walked out. He missed his children growing up. He missed funerals. He watched fellow prisoners die. The apartheid government wanted to break him, to make him irrelevant, to erase him from history.

Instead, he used those years. He studied his opponents, learning Afrikaans to understand the prison guards' conversations. He read their poetry, their history, their fears. He turned prison into a university, teaching fellow inmates. He learned to manage his anger, to separate the system from the individuals trapped within it. The valley didn't defeat him; it refined him.

When he finally emerged in 1990, he had every justification for vengeance. The crowds expected it. Some demanded it. But he'd transformed his 27 years of suffering into something the world desperately needed: a vision of reconciliation. He invited his former prison guard to his presidential inauguration. He wore the Springbok jersey—the symbol of apartheid oppression—to unite a fractured nation. He established the Truth and Reconciliation Commission, choosing healing over retribution.

His refusal to let bitterness win didn't just free South Africa from apartheid—it gave the world a new model for how societies can move beyond trauma. The wisdom he developed in that cell, the service he chose over rage, the breakthrough he achieved by refusing to become what oppressed him—none of it would exist without those 27 years in the valley.

This doesn't mean seeking out suffering but recognizing that when difficulties inevitably arise, we have opportunities to participate in the ancient human tradition of alchemy—transforming the lead of our challenges into the gold of wisdom and service.

The bamboo bends but doesn't break. The river flows around obstacles. The human spirit, when cultivated with wisdom and supported by community, reveals itself capable of transforming any adversity into a stepping stone toward greater consciousness and more authentic contribution.

This is resilience: not just surviving life's storms, but learning to dance with uncertainty, finding strength in flexibility, and discovering that we're far more bendable—and far more unbreakable—than we ever imagined.

Spiritual Practices that Cultivate Resilience

1. Journaling as Meaning-Making Writing is one of the most powerful tools of integration. When we write about our difficulties, we begin to organize chaos. We find patterns. We express what was previously stuck.

Keep a **resilience journal** with prompts like:

- What is life trying to teach me through this?
- What part of me is growing stronger?
- Who am I becoming through this challenge?

2. Meditation and Breathwork Stillness returns us to center. In stillness, we can watch our thoughts, observe our fear, and reconnect with the observer self—the *witness*.

Try this simple practice:

- Inhale slowly: *I am here.*

- Exhale slowly: *I can face this.*

3. Sacred Reading and Reframing Read sacred texts—not as dogma, but as **portals** into meaning. The Psalms, the Tao Te Ching, the Upanishads, or mystical poetry from Rumi, Rilke, Yeats, Hafiz, and Tagore.

Let these words **reshape your inner landscape**.

4. Nature Connection Nature is the oldest teacher. Observe how a tree sways in the storm, how seasons shift, how the forest recovers after fire. There is wisdom here. Be reminded that you, too, are nature.

5. Creative Expression Art, music, movement - all are ways to transmute emotion. Resilience increases when we have **outlets for expression**. You don't need to be good. You need to be real.

Cultural and Collective Resilience

Resilience is not only personal. It is also **collective**. Communities can cultivate resilience by telling the truth, holding each other in difficulty, sharing stories of survival and transformation.

Consider the **Jewish tradition of Passover**, retelling the story of liberation every year. Or the **African-American spirituals**, born in the crucible of slavery yet carrying hope.

When we gather in circle, when we share our truths, when we witness each other's journeys—we weave **a net of meaning**. And that net holds us.

Resilience in the Time of Chaotic Nodes

We are living through what many mystics and scientists call **"chaotic nodes"**—times when multiple systems are collapsing, and new patterns have not yet stabilized.

Natural disasters, political turmoil, economic volatility, social unrest, technological overwhelm, spiritual hunger—all happening **at once**.

It is easy to become cynical. Easy to collapse. But **this is precisely the moment resilience was made for.**

Hold the paradox. Do the next small thing. Trust the process.

Resilience is not the absence of difficulty. It is the art of **making something meaningful from it.**

Reflection Questions:

- What is one experience in my past that made me stronger?

- How do I respond to crisis: with fear, rigidity, or openness?

- What beliefs do I hold about suffering and its meaning?

- What spiritual or creative practices support my resilience?

Mantra: *I am shaped by events, not shattered by them. I make meaning from what meets me. I am resilient.*

Further Reading:

Pema Chödrön: *When Things Fall Apart*

Abraham Maslow: *Toward a Psychology of Being*

Viktor Frankl: *Man's Search for Meaning*

Admiral William H. McRaven: *Make your Bed*

Chapter 4: Sanctuary

Sacred Space for the Soul

"Silence is the sleep that nourishes wisdom." – Francis Bacon

"Be still, and know that I am God." - Psalm 46:10

There's something profound happening to us as a species, and I don't think we're talking about it enough. We're living in the first era in human history where silence has become genuinely rare. Where our attention is pulled in dozens of directions simultaneously. Where the ping of a notification can interrupt the deepest moments of reflection or connection.

In this cacophony of modern life, where digital raindrops of information threaten to wash away our inner peace like a technological tsunami, the ancient human need for sanctuary has transformed from luxury into necessity. Not just for mystics or monks, but for all of us trying to maintain our sanity and our souls in an age of perpetual stimulation.

The word "sanctuary" comes from the Latin *sanctuarium*, meaning "holy place," but its deeper meaning extends far beyond religious architecture. A sanctuary is any space—physical, mental, or spiritual—where we can withdraw from the demands of the world and reconnect with who we are beneath all the noise. It's where we can drop the performance of our social selves and simply be.

The Ancient Wisdom of Withdrawal

Throughout history, mystics and seekers have understood something we've largely forgotten: the soul needs space to breathe. The great monasteries and ashrams weren't built as escapes from life, but as laboratories for discovering what life truly means when stripped of superficial distractions.

The Desert Fathers and Mothers of early Christianity sought silence in the harsh stillness of wilderness places. Buddhist monks found clarity in mountain monasteries, far from the marketplace chatter. Hindu rishis sat by rivers or in mountain caves. The pattern is unmistakable: withdrawal allows for clarity, and clarity fosters wisdom.

These traditions understood what modern neuroscience now confirms: our brains need periods of non-stimulation to process information, integrate experiences, and access deeper levels of creativity and wisdom. When we're constantly responding to external stimuli, we never give our nervous systems the chance to settle. We are in a perpetual state of mental and emotional indigestion, finding it harder and harder to access what researchers call the "default mode network" - the brain state associated with introspection, moral reasoning, and identity formation.

Thomas Merton, the Trappist monk and mystic, captured this beautifully: "We do not go into the desert to escape people but to learn how to find them; we do not leave them in order to have nothing more to do with them, but to find out the way to do them the most good." This is sanctuary's true purpose: not withdrawal from life, but preparation for more authentic engagement with it.

Creating Sacred Space Anywhere

The beautiful truth about sanctuary is that it doesn't require dramatic escape or significant resources. It requires something far more accessible yet equally powerful: intention.

I converted a large closet in my home into a meditation room. It's small, simple, but it holds space for silence. A comfortable cushion, a candle, a few objects that carry personal meaning - nothing elaborate, but deeply intentional. It has become my threshold space, a room between worlds.

A friend who travels constantly for work carries what he calls his "traveling shrine" - a small wooden box containing photos, crystals, incense, a tiny cloth, and sacred images. Whether he's in a hotel room, an Airbnb, or conference center, he creates a mini-altar. It's his way of saying: "Spirit lives here too."

The power of such spaces lies not in their grandeur but in their consistency. When we repeatedly use the same objects and rituals to create sacred space, they become what psychologists call "contextual cues" - triggers that automatically shift our consciousness into a more receptive, peaceful state.

When you do have the opportunity to create a dedicated space at home, approach it as spiritual practice. Choose your location mindfully - ideally somewhere naturally quiet, away from main traffic patterns. The cleaning process becomes ritual: as you clear clutter and arrange the space, you're not just organizing physically but energetically.

The furnishing should reflect your personal spiritual path while maintaining simplicity. Natural elements—plants, stones, water—help connect your sanctuary to the larger web of life. Colors matter too: soft, natural tones generally promote peace, though there are no rigid rules. Scent often becomes the most powerful element, creating olfactory associations that will become linked with your spiritual practice.

The Inner Sanctum: Building Sacred Space Within

While physical sanctuaries are wonderful, perhaps the most important sacred space we can create exists within our own consciousness. The "inner sanctum" is a visualized refuge that remains available regardless of external circumstances.

Building this inner sanctuary begins with imagination but develops into something that feels utterly real and reliable. Here's how to create yours:

Choose Your Setting: Allow your imagination to explore different spaces that appeal to you. A cottage in an enchanted forest, a simple hut by the ocean, a cave in sacred mountains, a garden pavilion surrounded by flowering trees. There's no wrong choice - what matters is that it feels deeply peaceful and safe. Are you attracted to a particular geographical area? If you haven't been there yet, find some photographs and place your sacred space there. Maybe a hut made of palm fronds along the Nile?

Design the Architecture: Develop the structural elements. What does your sanctuary look like from outside? How do you approach it? Pay attention to materials and textures. Is it built of stone, wood, bamboo? Are there windows? What's the lighting like? These details create the sensory richness that makes your inner sanctum feel substantial. Through repetition of visualizing the space it will become increasingly clearer. Practice is key.

Create the Interior: Design for maximum comfort and spiritual connection. Include perfect seating - perhaps a comfortable chair, meditation cushions, or a simple bench. What objects populate this space? Books of wisdom, sacred symbols, musical instruments, crystals, flowers. Remember, this is imagination— you can include objects impossible in physical reality, like flowers that never fade.

Add Sensory Details: Make it vivid by including details for all senses. What does the air smell like? Perhaps sandalwood, ocean breezes, pine forests, blooming jasmine. What sounds are present? Wind chimes, distant waves, bird song, profound silence. What's the temperature? These details create the felt sense of actually being there.

Establish the Energy: Imbue your sanctuary with a particular quality of consciousness—profound peace, unconditional love, infinite wisdom, creative inspiration, healing energy. Imagine this as a palpable presence, perhaps appearing as golden light, flowing water, or simply the sense of being held by benevolent forces.

Practice Regularly: Visit your inner sanctum through meditation and visualization. Start with short visits and gradually extend them as the space becomes more familiar. With repeated practice, it will develop its own life and reality, often evolving naturally over time.

The Necessity of Recharge for Healers

If you work in any helping profession—therapy, teaching, healthcare, coaching, spiritual guidance - creating sanctuary becomes non-negotiable. You cannot pour from an empty vessel, and when we don't recharge, we begin to subtly extract energy from those we're trying to help.

This leads to burnout, even resentment of those we are trying to help, and to mechanical work devoid of the heart that originally called us to service. The great mystics and healers understood this: Jesus withdrew to the desert, Buddha meditated under the bodhi tree, Teresa of Avila emphasized solitude as essential to divine intimacy.

You don't need days of silence. Even fifteen minutes daily can shift your inner world. As Thomas Merton wrote, "There is a pervasive form of contemporary violence... activism and overwork. The frenzy of our activism neutralizes our work for peace."

Sacred Time and Digital Boundaries

Creating sanctuary isn't just about space - it's about time. Many traditions recognize sacred rhythms: the Jewish Sabbath creates weekly sanctuary in time, Islamic practice includes five daily prayer times, Christian monastics structure days around canonical hours. You don't need to adopt religious structures, but you do need some form of sacred rhythm.

In our digital age, one of sanctuary's most important aspects is establishing boundaries with technology. The constant stream of notifications creates chronic low-level stress our nervous systems weren't designed to handle. Digital fasting - temporarily disconnecting from devices—can be profoundly restorative.

Many people establish their sacred spaces as phone-free zones, recognizing that even device presence creates subtle tension. The blue light from screens disrupts both sleep and meditative states, while electromagnetic fields can create energetic disturbance.

For the Extroverts: Social Sanctuary

Not everyone thrives in solitude. Some find renewal through meaningful connection rather than withdrawal. If silence feels depleting rather than restorative, consider these heart-centered alternatives:

Join hiking groups where silence and awe emerge naturally. Sing in choirs - let harmony carry you. Volunteer at animal shelters, offering wordless care and receiving unconditional love. Serve at community kitchens or meals-on-wheels programs, finding presence through service.

The key is choosing activities that slow you down rather than speed you up, connect you to meaning rather than triviality, and leave you feeling centered rather than scattered.

Simple Practices for Deepening Sanctuary

Several practices can help cultivate and deepen your sanctuary experience:

Silence Practice: Begin with a few minutes daily. No music, phone, or input. Just sit, listen, breathe. Silence isn't the absence of sound but the presence of inner spaciousness.

Candle Meditation: Light a candle, sit before it, gaze softly at the flame. Let thoughts slow as flickering light reminds you of your own inner radiance.

Sacred Reading: The ancient Christian practice of *lectio divina*: reading spiritual texts slowly, reverently. Let words wash over you. Reflect on single lines. Savor meaning.

Breathwork or Mantra: Use simple mantras like "I am here" or "Peace surrounds me," or simply focus on breath. Inhale calm, exhale tension.

Anointing Ritual: Use essential oil on forehead or wrists before entering sanctuary. Let it symbolize transition into sacred time.

Sanctuary as Cultural Resistance

In our current moment, creating sanctuary has taken on profound significance. In a world profiting from our attention, distraction, and constant consumption, the decision to withdraw periodically and reconnect with our essential nature becomes an act of resistance.

When we take time to reconnect with our deepest values and clearest perception, we become more effective agents of positive change. When we refuse constant availability to external demands, we create space for authentic response rather than reactive behavior.

The creation of sanctuary becomes a practice of cultural healing. Every person who regularly retreats from modern hysteria and returns with greater clarity contributes to collective wellbeing. Every space dedicated to peace becomes a beacon of sanity in an increasingly chaotic world.

The Fruits of Sacred Practice

Regular sanctuary practice produces benefits extending far beyond the practice moments themselves. People report greater emotional stability, enhanced creativity, improved relationships, and deeper sense of purpose. Physiologically, it activates the parasympathetic nervous system—the "rest and digest" response allowing repair and regeneration.

Cognitively, sanctuary's space and silence allow for "diffuse attention" - a relaxed awareness promoting insight and creative breakthrough. Many find their best ideas emerge not during intense focus but during gentle, open awareness.

Most importantly, sanctuary practice helps us remember who we are beneath all roles and identities. In silence and space, we reconnect with our essential nature - that which remains constant beneath life's changes and challenges. This becomes an anchor sustaining us through difficulties and a source of authentic joy independent of circumstances.

Sanctuary is a Birthright

The world will not give you sanctuary—you must claim it. You were born to hold both outer storm and inner stillness. You're not here to be consumed by the world but to live from within outward, moving through life centered and grounded.

Make space. Make silence. Make your moments sacred. Even in the busiest city, even with chaos in the next room, you can light a candle in your heart. You can go there—to the sanctuary, the eternal one that waits for you.

As we learn to create and maintain sanctuary in our lives, we develop what might be called "sanctuary consciousness"—the ability to maintain inner peace and clarity regardless of external circumstances. This consciousness becomes portable, traveling with us into work, relationships, and daily activities, transforming not just our experience but the quality of presence we bring to everything we touch.

In a world hungry for authentic peace, every person who cultivates sanctuary consciousness becomes a gift to collective healing. The sanctuary you create for yourself becomes, in mysterious but real ways, a sanctuary for the world.

Mantra: *I am at home in myself.*

Chapter 5: Kindred Spirits

The Sacred Dance of Connection

"Where befriended paths meet, all the world seems for a moment like home." -Hermann Hesse

"No man is an island, entire of itself. Every man is a piece of the continent, a part of the main." -John Donne

Along with air, water and food, human beings need relationships to survive and thrive, and never more so than in turbulent times. The great mystery of human existence lies in the fact that our relationships simultaneously offer us our greatest opportunities for transcendence and our most exquisite forms of suffering. We are social creatures, wired for connection, yet cursed with the complex machinery of personality that makes authentic connection both desperately needed and maddeningly difficult.

In the grand theater of human experience, relationships serve as both the stage and the script, the actors and the audience. They are the mirrors in which we see ourselves most clearly—and most often, the reflections are not what we expected or particularly wanted to see. Yet it is precisely through these reflections that we have the opportunity to grow, to heal, and to discover the depths of our own capacity for love and understanding.

The Myth of Cosmic Assignment

Let's begin by addressing one of the most persistent myths of our time: the idea that we have no choice in where we're born or whom we encounter in this lifetime. Western culture, with its materialistic worldview, tends to see birth as a random biological accident - a cosmic lottery where consciousness accidentally ends up in this family, in this time, in this place, with these particular people as our involuntary companions for the journey.

But step outside this narrow perspective, and you'll find that virtually every metaphysical and spiritual tradition teaches something quite different. Whether we're talking about Tibetan Buddhism's concept of conscious rebirth, Hinduism's understanding of karmic contracts, the Sufi teaching of soul groups, or even certain interpretations of Plato's pre-existence of souls, the message is remarkably consistent: we don't just randomly tumble into relationships. We choose them.

Now, before you start protesting about your impossible mother-in-law or that ex who made your life a living hell, let's clarify what "choice" means in this context. We're not talking about the conscious, rational choice that your everyday personality makes when selecting a restaurant or a Netflix series. We're talking about the deeper wisdom of the soul, operating from a vantage point that encompasses multiple lifetimes and an understanding of what experiences will most effectively catalyze growth.

Think of it this way: if you were a soul attending "Earth University," and you needed to learn certain lessons—let's say patience, compassion, forgiveness, or the ability to maintain your center in chaos—wouldn't you choose professors who could really challenge you in those areas? From this perspective, that difficult parent, demanding boss, or turbulent romantic partner might actually be highly advanced souls who agreed to play the "heavy" in your personal growth drama.

This doesn't mean we should become doormats or tolerate abuse—discernment and healthy boundaries are also part of the curriculum. But it does suggest that we might approach our relationships with a bit more curiosity and a lot less victimhood when we recognize that, at some level, we signed up for this particular classroom.

The Single Soul Mate Delusion

Ah, the soul mate myth—perhaps Western culture's most romantic and simultaneously most limiting belief about relationships. According to this popular narrative, somewhere out there in the vast cosmos is your "other half," the one person who will complete you, understand you perfectly, and transform your life into a fairy tale of perpetual bliss. Jerry Maguire had us all swooning with "You complete me," and we've been chasing that completeness ever since, often with the desperation of someone looking for their missing shoe while already late for work.

This single soul mate doctrine creates enormous pressure on our relationships. One poor human being is expected to be lover, best friend, therapist, entertainment committee, spiritual teacher, and cosmic twin all rolled into one perfectly compatible package. It's no wonder that divorce rates soar when real people inevitably fail to live up to these impossible expectations.

The reality is far more interesting and, paradoxically, more romantic than the Hollywood version. If we accept that consciousness is vast, multifaceted, and capable of expressing itself through countless forms, then why would our spiritual connections be limited to just one other person? That would be like saying a symphony orchestra should consist of only two instruments playing the same note.

Consider instead the possibility that love is not a scarce resource to be hoarded between two people, but an abundant energy that can flow between many souls in many different forms. Your soul mate might be your best friend from childhood who sees right through your pretenses and loves you anyway. It might be the teacher who recognized your potential when you couldn't see it yourself. It might be the child who chose you as a parent, bringing lessons about unconditional love and patience. It might even be that difficult colleague who triggers all your buttons and forces you to develop emotional mastery.

When we expand our understanding of soul connections beyond the narrow confines of romantic partnership, we begin to recognize the rich tapestry of meaningful relationships that surround us. We stop putting impossible pressure on our romantic partners to be everything to us, and we start appreciating the diverse ways that love shows up in our lives.

The Kabbalistic Vision: A Light Divided

Jewish mysticism offers one of the most beautiful and comprehensive understandings of soul connections through its teaching about the fragmentation and reunion of divine light. According to Kabbalistic tradition, there was originally one unified soul-light, perfect and whole. But in order for this light to experience itself, to grow and evolve, it had to be divided into individual sparks—each carrying the memory of the original unity but also the yearning to rediscover it.

Some teachings speak of as many as eighty or more soul fragments that originated from the same source light. These fragments, scattered across time and space, naturally recognize each other when they meet. It's that immediate sense of familiarity you sometimes feel with a stranger, the inexplicable comfort you experience in certain people's presence, or the feeling that you've known someone forever even though you just met.

This Kabbalistic understanding explains why soul connections can take so many forms. Your soul fragments might incarnate as your parent, child, sibling, friend, teacher, student, or romantic partner in different lifetimes. The connection transcends the specific role and speaks to the deeper recognition of shared essence.

I remember years ago seeing an interview with Richard Gere talking about the birth of his first son. He was telling the story of when he held him for the first time in the hospital immediately after he was born. His first words were "oh, it's you again". There was an instant recognition of something intangible, of a kindred soul. "I remember you."

This understanding also explains why some relationships feel immediately easy and natural while others require more work. Soul fragments that have traveled together for many lifetimes might slip into comfortable, supportive connection with minimal friction. Others might be meeting for the first time in centuries and need to relearn how to harmonize their energies.

But here's where it gets really interesting: according to this tradition, we're not just randomly bumping into our soul family members. There's a higher organizing intelligence that orchestrates these meetings for maximum growth and healing potential. You might encounter a soul sibling at exactly the moment when you both need what the other has to offer, or reconnect with an old soul friend just as you're ready to learn a lesson they can teach.

The Personality Predicament

Now, here's where the plot thickens. Even if we accept that we're all divine sparks of light seeking reunion with our cosmic family, we still have to contend with the rather stubborn fact that we're currently wearing these elaborate costumes called personalities - and some of these costumes are, frankly, a bit much.

None of us arrived on Earth as blank slates, *tabula rasa* as the Latins used to call it, despite what the philosopher John Locke might have argued. (Though to be fair, Locke probably never had to deal with online dating or family holiday dinners, so we'll cut him some slack.) We each come equipped with our own unique combination of gifts and neuroses, light and shadow, charming quirks and maddening habits.

Your soul mate might be the most compatible energetic match imaginable, but if their personality happens to include, say, an inability to close kitchen cabinets or a tendency to leave towels on the bathroom floor, you're going to have some very earthly challenges to navigate. The soul recognizes the soul, but the personality has to live with the personality—and personalities are notoriously unreasonable creatures.

This is where relationships become our most intensive workshops for personal development. It's relatively easy to be spiritual, evolved, and compassionate when you're alone on a mountaintop meditation retreat. It's considerably more challenging when your beloved soul companion has just used the last of the coffee without making more, left their dishes in the sink again, and somehow managed to lose the car keys for the third time this week.

The French playwright Jean Anouilh wisely observed, "Love is, above all else, the gift of oneself." But what he didn't mention is that sometimes the person you're giving yourself to would rather you kept some parts of yourself to yourself, thank you very much. This is where the spiritual rubber meets the psychological road. Jean-Paul Sartre, the French existentialist philosopher, summed it up with a few words: "Hell is…other people!"

Attracted to Our Own Blocks

During my training as a therapist, my supervisor shared an insight that has proven to be both illuminating and occasionally terrifying: we are magnetically drawn to our own emotional blocks, especially in intimate relationships. It's as if our unconscious minds have some kind of internal radar system specifically calibrated to detect people who will activate our deepest wounds and most stubborn patterns.

This might seem like a cruel cosmic joke at first glance. Why would the universe be so mean as to make us fall in love with people who push all our buttons? But when viewed through the lens of growth and healing, it's actually quite ingenious. Our emotional blocks are like psychological muscles that have become frozen and weak from disuse. They need to be exercised, stretched, and sometimes even torn down and rebuilt in order to become healthy.

A person who grew up with an emotionally distant parent might find themselves consistently attracted to partners who are loving but have their own challenges with emotional availability. Someone who learned to suppress their anger in childhood might be drawn to partners who express anger freely—perhaps too freely. The workaholic might fall for the free spirit, the pessimist for the eternal optimist, the controller for the chaos creator.

At the personality level, these attractions can feel like disasters waiting to happen. And sometimes they are—at least in the short term. But from the soul's perspective, they're golden opportunities for integration and wholeness. The parts of us that we've rejected, suppressed, or never learned to develop can be awakened through relationship with someone who embodies those qualities.

This doesn't mean we should stay in relationships that are genuinely harmful or abusive. Discernment is crucial. But it does suggest that we might approach relationship challenges with more curiosity and less immediate judgment. Instead of asking "Why did I end up with this impossible person?" we might ask "What is this relationship trying to teach me? What part of myself am I being invited to develop or heal?"

The novelist Marcel Proust captured this beautifully: "The real voyage of discovery consists not in seeking new landscapes, but in having new eyes." Sometimes the greatest journey we can take is seeing our familiar relationship patterns through the lens of growth rather than victimhood.

Soul Mates vs. Karma Mates

This brings us to a crucial distinction that I've found invaluable in understanding the different types of connections we experience: the difference between soul mates and karma mates. While both types of relationships involve deep soul connections, they serve very different purposes in our spiritual evolution.

A true soul mate relationship tends to feel relatively easy and natural, even when it includes challenges. There's a fundamental harmony between the souls that allows for authentic expression, mutual support, and shared growth. Conflicts in soul mate relationships usually resolve fairly quickly because both people are fundamentally committed to love and understanding. These relationships often feel like coming home to yourself. Ram Dass sums it up beautifully: "We are all just walking each other home."

Karma mate relationships, on the other hand, are specifically designed for healing and transformation. They tend to be more intense, more challenging, and more emotionally triggering. These are the relationships that activate your deepest wounds, challenge your most cherished defense mechanisms, and force you to confront parts of yourself you'd rather ignore.

Karma mate relationships are not necessarily meant to last forever, though some do. Their primary purpose is to catalyze growth and healing. Sometimes this work can be completed, and the relationship naturally evolves or ends with gratitude. Other times, the healing happens within the context of an ongoing partnership, leading to deeper intimacy and understanding.

The key is recognizing which type of relationship you're in and adjusting your expectations accordingly. If you're expecting a karma mate relationship to feel like a soul mate connection, you're going to be frustrated and disappointed. But if you can recognize the karma mate dynamic for what it is - a powerful opportunity for healing and growth - you can work with it more skillfully.

I once had a client who described her marriage this way: "I used to think I married the wrong person because it was so hard. Then I realized I married exactly the right person because it was so hard. He's been my greatest teacher, even when I wanted to throw things at him." That's karma mate wisdom in action.

The Cosmic Curriculum of Connection

When we begin to see our relationships as part of a larger curriculum for soul development, everything shifts. Instead of seeing difficult people as obstacles to our happiness, we start recognizing them as teachers offering advanced courses in patience, compassion, forgiveness, and emotional mastery.

This perspective doesn't mean we become passive or accept poor treatment. In fact, it often requires us to develop stronger boundaries, clearer communication, and more authentic self-expression. The curriculum of connection includes learning to love without losing yourself, to be compassionate without becoming a doormat, and to forgive without condoning harmful behavior.

Consider the parent who triggers your deepest insecurities. From a karmic perspective, this might be exactly the teacher you need to develop unshakeable self-worth. The demanding boss might be offering you a masterclass in maintaining your center under pressure. The friend who consistently disappoints you might be teaching you about realistic expectations and self-reliance.

Of course, this is much easier to see in retrospect than in the moment. When you're in the midst of relationship drama, it's hard to appreciate the cosmic curriculum. But developing the ability to pause and ask, "What might this be trying to teach me?" can transform even the most challenging relationship dynamics.

The playwright Tennessee Williams wrote, "The only thing worse than not getting what you want is someone else getting it." But I would add: the only thing more transformative than getting what you want is discovering what you actually need through the people who challenge you most.

The Familiar Strangers

One of the most mysterious aspects of human connection is the phenomenon of instant recognition - meeting someone and immediately feeling like you've known them forever. This can happen in romantic contexts, but it's just as likely to occur with a new friend, a teacher, or even someone you meet briefly in passing.

These moments of recognition often transcend logical explanation. You might meet someone whose background is completely different from yours, whose personality seems quite unlike your own, yet something in you immediately says, "I know you." It's not physical attraction, though that might also be present. It's something deeper - a resonance at the level of essence.

From the perspective of reincarnation and soul groups, these recognitions make perfect sense. You're encountering someone with whom you've shared significant experiences in previous lifetimes. The soul remembers, even when the personality doesn't. It's like bumping into an old college roommate at a conference twenty years later—there's an immediate warmth and familiarity that transcends the time and changes that have passed.

But here's the interesting thing: these soul recognitions don't automatically guarantee easy relationships. Sometimes you recognize someone precisely because you have unfinished business with them. That immediate magnetic pull might be your souls saying, "Oh good, here's our chance to finally work through that thing we've been avoiding for three lifetimes." I have observed in decades on this Earth, that often the people we have important unfinished business with are the ones we fall the hardest and the fastest for. It's like the Universe uses an extra dose of crazy glue to make sure we stay together long enough to finish whatever lesson is on the menu.

I have a friend who describes meeting her now-husband as feeling like she was being "called home by someone I'd been homesick for without knowing it." They've had a beautiful, supportive marriage for fifteen years. But I have another friend who felt instant recognition when she met someone who turned out to be one of the most challenging relationships of her life - a beautiful but ultimately impossible connection that taught her profound lessons about love, attachment, and letting go.

The recognition itself is always meaningful, but the form the relationship takes can vary enormously based on what healing and growth is needed.

The Art of Loving Difficult People

If we're going to talk honestly about relationships, we need to address a fundamental challenge: some people are genuinely difficult to love. Not because they're evil or worthless, but because their personalities, defense mechanisms, and ways of being in the world clash with our own in ways that generate friction, frustration, and sometimes real pain.

Traditional spiritual teachings often make this sound easier than it is. "Just love everyone," they say. "See the divine in all beings." "Practice unconditional compassion." These are beautiful ideals, but they can feel like spiritual bypassing when you're dealing with someone whose idea of communication is passive-aggressive manipulation or whose emotional regulation skills peaked somewhere around age four.

The art of loving difficult people requires tremendous skill and discernment. It means learning to separate the soul from the personality, to respond to essence rather than just reacting to behavior. It means developing compassion for the wounds and fears that drive difficult behavior while still maintaining appropriate boundaries.

This is particularly challenging with family members, whom we didn't choose (at least not consciously) and whom we can't easily remove from our lives. That relative who always has something critical to say, the sibling who never grew out of their adolescent drama patterns, the parent who still treats you like a child despite your being a successful adult—these relationships test our capacity for unconditional love like nothing else.

Buddhist teacher Pema Chödrön offers a helpful reframe: instead of trying to love difficult people despite their challenging qualities, we can practice loving them because of what they teach us. That demanding relative might be offering you a masterclass in patience. The critical family member might be helping you develop unshakeable self-worth. The chaotic friend might be teaching you about maintaining your center in the midst of other people's storms.

This doesn't mean we have to spend unlimited time with difficult people or accept harmful behavior. Love sometimes means saying no, setting boundaries, or even choosing to love someone from a distance. The poet Rainer Maria Rilke wrote, "Love consists in this: that two solitudes protect and border and greet each other." Sometimes the most loving thing we can do is to honor both our own and others' need for space.

The Unexpected Teachers

Some of our most profound teachers come in forms we never expected. The child who chooses you as a parent and proceeds to dismantle every assumption you had about yourself. The boss who seems impossible but forces you to develop professional skills you never knew you needed. The stranger who offers kindness at exactly the moment you need it most.

I once knew a woman who described her teenage son as her greatest spiritual teacher: "He's shown me depths of patience I never knew I had, and also limits to that patience that I needed to acknowledge. He's taught me about unconditional love and appropriate consequences, about holding space for someone's growth while not enabling their poor choices. I used to think I was supposed to teach him about life, but it turns out he came to teach me about love."

These unexpected teacher relationships remind us that spiritual growth doesn't always come in the packages we expect. Sometimes enlightenment arrives wearing dirty sneakers and asking to borrow money. Sometimes wisdom speaks with an accent we have trouble understanding. Sometimes love shows up in the form of someone who challenges everything we thought we knew about ourselves.

The key is staying open to these unexpected forms of teaching. When we get too attached to how we think growth should look or where wisdom should come from, we might miss the profound lessons being offered by the people right in front of us.

The Dance of Projection and Recognition

One of the most complex aspects of relationships is the interplay between projection and genuine recognition. We're constantly projecting our own inner material onto others—seeing our own fears, desires, wounds, and potentials reflected in the people around us. But we're also genuinely recognizing soul connections and authentic qualities in others.

Learning to distinguish between projection and recognition is one of the great skills of conscious relationship. When you feel instantly drawn to someone, is it because you recognize a kindred soul, or because they're embodying some aspect of yourself that you've lost touch with? When someone irritates you intensely, are you responding to their actual behavior, or are they triggering some unresolved aspect of your own psychology?

The answer is usually "both." Most relationships involve a complex mixture of projection and recognition, karma and soul connection, personal psychology and spiritual purpose. The work is learning to sort these different levels and respond to each appropriately.

Carl Jung wrote, "Everything that irritates us about others can lead us to an understanding of ourselves." This is particularly true in close relationships, where our projections are most intense and most revelatory. The qualities we admire in others often point to our own undeveloped potentials. The traits we find most annoying in others frequently highlight our own shadow material.

But Jung also recognized that sometimes we're simply recognizing authentic qualities in others, both positive and negative. The skill is in learning to discern when we're seeing clearly and when we're seeing through the lens of our own psychological material.

Practical Wisdom for Navigating Soul Connections

Given all this complexity, how do we navigate relationships with both spiritual awareness and practical wisdom? Here are some principles I've found helpful:

Listen to Your Heart, but Engage Your Head: That immediate soul recognition is valuable information, but it's not the whole picture. Pay attention to both the spiritual resonance and the practical compatibility. A soul connection doesn't automatically mean this person should be your roommate, business partner, or life companion.

Expect Growth, Not Perfection: Every person you're in relationship with is a work in progress, just as you are. Hold space for growth and change rather than expecting anyone (including yourself) to be finished products.

Practice Discernment: Not every spiritual lesson requires you to stay and work through it within the relationship. Sometimes the lesson is about learning to leave, set boundaries, or love from a distance. Trust your inner guidance about when to stay and when to go.

Look for Patterns: If you find yourself repeatedly attracting the same type of challenging relationship, pay attention. Your soul might be trying to work through a particular pattern or lesson. Instead of just changing partners, consider what internal work might break the cycle.

Appreciate the Teachers: Even difficult relationships serve purposes. Practice gratitude (perhaps from a safe distance) for what each person has taught you, even if the lessons were painful.

Stay Open to Surprise: Some of your most meaningful connections might not look like what you expected. Don't get so focused on finding your "type" that you miss the kindred spirits who come in unexpected packaging.

As we come to understand relationships as part of a larger spiritual curriculum, we can approach them with more wisdom, patience, and appreciation. We can love more deeply because we understand that love includes the whole messy, beautiful, challenging process of souls helping each other grow.

The poet Adrienne Rich wrote, "There must be those among whom we can sit down and weep and still be counted as warriors." These are your true kindred spirits—not necessarily the people who never challenge you, but the ones with whom you can be completely authentic, who see your full humanity and love you not despite it but because of it.

In the end, we are all just walking each other home, as Ram Dass said. Some companions make the journey feel easy and joyful. Others challenge us to develop strength and wisdom we never knew we had. All of them, in their own way, are serving the great work of love—helping us remember who we really are beneath the costumes of personality, and supporting us in becoming the fullest, most authentic versions of ourselves.

The great secret is that there is no single soul mate waiting out there to complete you. You are already complete. The relationships that come into your life—soul mates and karma mates alike—are not there to fill your emptiness but to help you discover the fullness that was always there. They are mirrors, teachers, playmates, and fellow travelers on the great adventure of conscious awakening.

And sometimes, if you're very lucky, they remember to make coffee before they leave for work.

Reflection Prompts: Are my relationships allowing me to become a better version of myself? How do certain qualities in my friends and family that I still reject represent projections of parts of myself I am still struggling with? What would those relationships look like if I took back my projections? Are there patterns that keep on repeating themselves in my relationships?

Mantra: *I am a work in progress. My relationships are my learning ground.*

Further Reading:

Tara Brach: *Nourishing Intimacy*

Caroline Myss: *Sacred Contracts*

Dr. Michael Newton: *Destiny of Souls*

Dr. Harriet Lerner: *The Dance of Connection*

Chapter 6: Imaginatio

The Divine Creative Force

"Imagination is more important than knowledge. For knowledge is limited to all we now know and understand, while imagination embraces the entire world, and all there ever will be to know and understand." - Albert Einstein

"Happiness is not an ideal of reason, but of imagination." – Immanuel Kant

Every moment of every day, you are creating. Not just in obvious ways—through words, actions, or artistic endeavors—but through the constant stream of internal imagery flowing through your consciousness like an endless river. From waking until sleep, and beyond into dreams, you generate a continuous cascade of mental images connected to wishes, fears, hopes, memories, and expectations of the future.

This faculty of imagination, which Renaissance alchemists called *Imaginatio*, represents one of humanity's most profound and least understood superpowers. It bridges visible and invisible worlds, serves as the mechanism through which consciousness shapes reality, and provides the tool for transcending ordinary perception to explore infinite possibilities of existence.

Yet we've largely relegated imagination to entertainment and childhood fantasy, failing to recognize its immense power to shape reality. We dismiss internal images as "just imagination," not realizing these creations have power to heal or harm, liberate or imprison, connect us with deepest truths or trap us in self-made illusions.

The Constant Creation

Consider the sheer volume of imagery flowing through your consciousness daily. You wake generating images of your day ahead—visualizing commutes, imagining conversations, picturing task completions. You recall yesterday's experiences, replay pleasant moments, ruminate on difficulties. You create scenarios of possible futures, both desired and feared.

This process is so natural we rarely consider its significance. Yet each internal image carries emotional charge, affects physiology, influences decisions, and literally shapes reality experience. Pleasant visualizations trigger pleasure physiology. Threatening images activate stress responses as if threats were real.

The mother waiting for her teenage child doesn't simply worry abstractly. Her imagination creates vivid accident scenes, emergency scenarios, detailed danger visions. These entirely self-generated images trigger genuine stress hormones and create real suffering—all for events existing nowhere but imagination. Similarly, discovering an unknown text on a partner's phone immediately sparks elaborate betrayal fantasies, detailed infidelity narratives that can produce intense jealousy despite being fictional creations.

This demonstrates both incredible power and potential danger of untrained imagination. Like a runaway vehicle with tremendous horsepower but no steering, uncontrolled imagination can create havoc, generating unnecessary suffering, distorting reality perception, and trapping us in self-made prisons.

The Modern Image Bombardment

Our contemporary digital age has exponentially complicated this situation. Never have people been exposed to such constant external imagery bombardment. Television, internet, social media, advertising, streaming services, video games, and countless sources pour endless image streams into consciousness daily.

These external images don't remain passive; they interact with internal imagination, seeding minds with content we unconsciously incorporate into our own image-making process. Violent movie scenes appear in anxiety-driven fantasies. Advertising's idealized bodies become standards we measure ourselves against, often finding reality disappointing compared to digitally manipulated fabrications.

Social media has created entirely new imaginative distortions. We see carefully curated life highlights and our imagination fills narrative gaps, creating stories about others' wonderful, successful, happy lives. We compare these fabricated narratives with unfiltered reality of our inner experience, inevitably finding actual lives disappointing compared to imaginary ones.

We've become largely unconscious of this process, absorbing external images passively, allowing them to shape internal landscapes without conscious choice, then wondering why we feel anxious, inadequate, or disconnected from reality.

The Neuroscience of Imagined Reality

Modern neuroscience validates what mystics have understood for millennia: the brain cannot distinguish between vividly imagined experiences and actual events regarding physiological and emotional responses. Imagining biting a fresh lemon triggers mouth-watering exactly as eating actual fruit. Visualizing successful presentations activates the same neural networks as actually delivering speeches.

This neurological reality has profound implications. Every mental image we create is, in a very real sense, an experienced reality. Jealous partner scenarios trigger identical stress responses to witnessing actual betrayal. Success fantasies generate genuine accomplishment feelings matching real achievement.

Functional MRI studies show that imagining specific physical actions activates motor cortex regions associated with those actions, despite no physical movement occurring. Olympic athletes use this principle, spending hours mentally rehearsing performances with such vividness that bodies literally practice visualized movements. This research reveals imagination not as mere fantasy, but as fundamental mechanism through which consciousness interfaces with and shapes physical reality.

The Egyptian Mystery Temples

Ancient Egyptian temple complexes served not merely as worship places but as sophisticated consciousness transformation centers through guided imagery. The famous underground chambers beneath Giza, intricate pyramid passages, and temple sanctuaries throughout Egypt were designed as environments for inducing altered states through carefully orchestrated imaginal experiences.

Initiates underwent elaborate death-and-rebirth visualizations in pyramid depths, experiencing dissolution and reconstitution as transformed beings. Hieroglyphic texts describe detailed underworld journeys, divine encounters, and spiritual purification processes experienced through directed imagination—not mere beliefs but actual consciousness explorations through inner vision power.

The Eleusinian Mysteries

The Greek Mystery School at Eleusis represents perhaps history's most famous example of using imagery for spiritual transformation. For over two millennia, people from across the Mediterranean traveled to participate in secret rites promising profound spiritual revelation through direct experience.

While exact ritual details remain hidden, historical accounts suggest carefully orchestrated dramatic presentations combined with consciousness-altering substances enabling vivid visions of death, rebirth, and divine communion. Participants didn't simply hear Demeter and Persephone's story; they experienced it as personal journey, using imagination to traverse realms of death and rebirth, emerging transformed with direct immortality knowledge.

The Asclepian Healing Temples

Greek Asclepius temples developed perhaps the most sophisticated ancient system for therapeutic imagination use. These healing centers throughout the Greek world functioned as places where people with physical and psychological ailments sought divine intervention through dream incubation.

The process was remarkably sophisticated. After ritual purification, seekers slept in special temple chambers called *abaton*. During sleep, they received healing visions from Asclepius or divine assistants. These weren't hopeful dreams but structured imaginal experiences often resulting in dramatic healings, with temple records documenting thousands of cases where people with chronic conditions experienced complete recovery following visionary encounters.

The Asclepian approach recognized that healing imagery must emerge from individuals' own psyches rather than being externally imposed. Priests facilitated conditions where seekers' imagination could access needed healing wisdom. This ancient understanding resonates with modern films like Christopher Nolan's "Inception," which explores how dreams can be therapeutic spaces for psychological transformation and healing, though the film focuses more on implanting ideas than allowing natural healing wisdom to emerge.

Taoist Inner Alchemy

Chinese Taoist tradition developed systematic approaches to imagination for spiritual development through *neidan* or inner alchemy practices. These involved elaborate visualizations designed to transform practitioners' internal energy and consciousness, imagining internal organs as palace complexes inhabited by divine beings and energy circulating through specific body pathways.

The famous Taoist "internal landscape" practice involved mapping the body as mountainous terrain with rivers, temples, and spiritual beings, using imagination to explore and transform this inner world. These weren't symbolic exercises but practical techniques for directing life force energy and achieving the "immortal body" - consciousness transcending ordinary physical limitations.

The Hermetic Tradition

The Hermetic tradition, emerging from Greek philosophy and Egyptian mystery wisdom synthesis, developed sophisticated theoretical frameworks for understanding imagination's creative power. The fundamental principle "as above, so below" refers to the creative relationship between consciousness and reality, with imagination serving as the connecting link.

Hermetic practitioners understood imagination (*imaginatio*) as the faculty through which human consciousness participates in ongoing reality creation. Renaissance figures like Paracelsus,

Agrippa, and Bruno developed these insights into practical systems for healing, divination, and consciousness expansion, understanding that properly trained imagination could influence not only personal experience but reality's broader fabric.

Christian Mystical Traditions

Christian mysticism developed sophisticated approaches to sacred imagery, though often hidden within orthodox theological language. The tradition of *lectio divina* involved using imagination to enter Biblical scenes and experience them as personal spiritual realities. Saints like Ignatius of Loyola developed elaborate systems for prayer and contemplation imagination use.

The Ignatian Spiritual Exercises involve placing oneself imaginally within Gospel scenes, experiencing sights, sounds, smells, and emotional atmosphere of Christ's life. These practices create genuine divine communion through imagination's gateway, understanding it as direct communication means with God when purified of ego-driven desires.

Particularly significant in this tradition is the work of Daskalos (Dr. Stylianos Atteshlis), the Cypriot mystic and healer whose teachings on visualization revolutionized understanding of consciousness mechanics. Daskalos taught that every thought creates distinct energetic forms continuing to exist after thoughts pass from conscious awareness, and that through love, understanding, and forgiveness, even deeply ingrained negative thought patterns could be consciously transformed. His systematic approach to visualization—creating healing images, communicating with higher spiritual planes, and using imagination for spiritual elevation—demonstrated practical applications of Christian mystical principles. Daskalos emphasized that imagination properly directed becomes a vehicle for divine grace, enabling practitioners to experience direct spiritual realities and participate consciously in cosmic healing processes.

Carl Gustav Jung and Active Imagination

Carl Jung revolutionized modern psychology's understanding of imagination through Active Imagination development, recognizing that psyche constantly produces imagery seeking integration. Rather than interpreting images intellectually, Jung encouraged direct engagement as if they were autonomous beings.

Jung discovered that authentic engagement with inner imagery—conversing with dream figures, exploring imaginal landscapes, allowing internal dramas to unfold—produced profound psychological healing. Complexes creating symptoms began resolving, blocked creative energies flowed again, and individuals accessed previously unknown wisdom and resources.

Jung's approach was revolutionary in recognizing inner images as connections to the "collective unconscious"—universal patterns shared by humanity. His personal work, documented in *The Red Book*, chronicles his own descent into imagination's depths, engaging with archetypal figures and recording visionary experiences that shaped his psychological theories. Through Active Imagination, individuals could access not only personal healing resources but tap into entire species wisdom traditions, demonstrating imagination as genuine faculty for consciousness exploration rather than mere fantasy.

Shamanic Journeying: Harner and Wesselman

The late twentieth century saw remarkable developments in shamanic practice revival for modern therapeutic use. Michael Harner, trained as an anthropologist, spent decades studying indigenous shamanic traditions worldwide, revealing that beneath surface diversity lay common core practices involving drumming, rattling, and other techniques for inducing altered states where practitioners could access non-ordinary reality through imagination power.

Harner developed "core shamanism"—a distilled approach safely usable by modern people without appropriating specific indigenous traditions. Central to this is the shamanic journey, where participants use repetitive drumming as sonic vehicle for consciousness to travel in imagination to the "spirit world," encountering power animals, spirit guides, and non-ordinary beings providing healing, guidance, and information unavailable to ordinary consciousness.

Hank Wesselman, evolutionary biologist turned shamanic practitioner, extended this work by documenting extraordinary journeys into "expanded reality." Wesselman's experiences suggest that consciousness, properly directed through imagination, can transcend spatial and temporal limitations, accessing information from past and future time periods.

Wesselman's accounts of journeying to future time periods, encountering advanced human consciousnesses, and receiving information about humanity's evolutionary potential demonstrate imagination's capacity to transcend ordinary space-time limitations. His work suggests what we call imagination may actually be natural faculty for consciousness exploration suppressed by materialistic worldviews, opening possibilities for genuine time travel and interdimensional communication through properly cultivated imaginative practices.

The Infinite Canvas of Possibility

Understanding imagination's true nature reveals we're dealing with consciousness's fundamental creative force. Imagination isn't separate from reality but the very mechanism through which reality is continuously created. When properly understood and consciously directed, imagination becomes a tool for healing, transformation, and exploring realities beyond physical limitations.

Want to explore Mars's surface? Imagination can transport you there with vividness that consciousness genuinely experiences alien landscapes. Curious about ancient Egypt? Through imagination, walk Karnak temple halls, sail the Nile, participate in mystery initiations. Modern physics suggests reality itself may be more imaginal than previously understood, with quantum mechanics demonstrating that consciousness influences physical reality through observation.

Practices for Conscious Creation

Understanding imagination's power is only the beginning. The key is developing practices that allow us to work consciously and skillfully with this creative force rather than being at the mercy of its unconscious expressions.

The Daily Image Inventory

Begin by developing awareness of your constant image-making activity. Several times throughout each day, pause and ask yourself: "What images have been flowing through my consciousness in the past hour? What am I visualizing about my future? What memories am I replaying? What scenarios am I creating about other people's actions or motivations?"

Simply becoming conscious of this constant stream of imagery is the first step toward working with it skillfully. You might be surprised to discover how much of your mental energy is devoted to creating images that generate stress, anxiety, or other negative states.

The Reality Check Practice

When you notice yourself becoming emotionally reactive to a situation, pause and ask: "What images am I creating about this situation? How much of my reaction is based on what's actually happening versus what I'm imagining might be happening?" I came across this wonderful quote recently by French philosopher Michel de Montaigne: "My life has been full of terrible misfortunes, most of which never happened". Laugh at yourself , that will instantly raise your frequency!

Conscious Image Replacement

Once you identify destructive or unhelpful imagery patterns, practice consciously replacing them with more beneficial images. If you find yourself constantly visualizing worst-case scenarios, deliberately practice creating best-case images instead. If you're replaying painful memories, practice reimagining those situations with different outcomes or from perspectives of forgiveness and understanding. Some time ago I became obsessed with a very unpleasant image of a worse-case health scenario. After fighting it for a few days I started to visualize this beautiful multi-colored butterfly every time the negative image would arise. Shortly afterward the recurring negative image disappeared.

This isn't about denying reality or engaging in wishful thinking, but about recognizing that you have choice in what you create in your imagination and that these creations profoundly influence your experience.

Dialogue with Inner Figures

Following Jung's Active Imagination approach, practice engaging in conversation with figures that appear in your dreams or meditation. Rather than analyzing these figures, interact with them directly. Ask them questions, listen to their responses, and develop ongoing relationships with helpful inner allies.

These figures often represent aspects of your own wisdom and creativity that aren't accessible to your ordinary conscious mind. Through dialogue, you can access guidance, healing energy, and creative inspiration that emerge from deeper levels of your own consciousness.

Future Self Consultation

Use imagination to connect with your future self—the person you'll be when you've grown, healed, and developed in the ways you're seeking. Visualize this future self in detail and practice having conversations with them. What advice would they give you about your current challenges? What do they know that you're still learning? Write a letter to your future self.

This practice accesses your own potential wisdom while also programming your unconscious mind with images of positive development and growth.

Healing Imagery Work

Develop specific imagery practices for supporting your physical and emotional health. This might involve visualizing your immune system as warrior allies fighting infection, imagining healing light flowing through areas of pain or tension, or seeing yourself in states of perfect health and vitality.

The key is making these images as vivid and emotionally compelling as possible, engaging not just visual imagination but all your senses in creating the healing experience.

The Sacred Responsibility

As we develop our imaginative faculties, we must also develop responsibility for how we use this power. Every image we create contributes to the overall field of human consciousness. When we generate images of fear, violence, or separation, we're adding these energies to the collective human experience. When we create images of love, healing, and unity, we're contributing to humanity's positive evolution.

This responsibility extends to how we engage with external imagery as well. The images we choose to consume through media, the fantasies we indulge in, the mental scenarios we create about others - all of these have energetic consequences that extend beyond our personal experience.

Conscious practitioners learn to ask themselves: "What kind of images am I contributing to the world? Are my visualizations and fantasies serving the highest good, or are they feeding destructive patterns in myself and humanity?"

This doesn't mean becoming rigid or joyless about imagination, but rather developing discernment about how to use this sacred creative power in ways that serve healing, growth, and the evolution of consciousness.

A Practical Prompt for Exploration

The Healing Journey Visualization

Find a comfortable position where you won't be disturbed for 20-30 minutes. Close your eyes and take several deep breaths, feeling your body relax more with each exhale.

Begin by visiting your inner sanctuary - that place of perfect peace and safety that exists in your imagination. Spend a few minutes making this space vivid and real, engaging all your senses in the experience.

From your sanctuary, notice a path leading into beautiful natural surroundings. This might be a forest path, a mountain trail, a beach walk, or any natural setting that calls to you. Begin walking along this path with curiosity and openness.

As you walk, you notice that the landscape around you seems to reflect your inner emotional and energetic state. Areas that appear dark, tangled, or harsh represent aspects of yourself that need healing attention. Areas that appear bright, flowing, or beautiful represent your healthy, vital energies.

Choose one area that seems to need healing attention and approach it with compassion. You might find a wounded animal, a dried-up stream, a withered tree, or any image that represents what needs healing in your life.

Now call upon a healing presence to join you. This might be a wise grandmother figure, an angel, a plant or nature spirit, an animal guide, or any being that represents healing wisdom to you. Allow this being to appear and offer their assistance.

Work together with your healing ally to restore the wounded area. You might offer the wounded creature medicine, tend to it with loving care, clear debris from a blocked stream, or nurture new growth in barren soil. Allow your imagination to show you exactly what's needed.

As the healing work progresses, notice how the landscape transforms. See the area becoming more vibrant, alive, and beautiful. Feel the energy shifting from depletion to vitality, from pain to wholeness.

When the healing feels complete, thank your healing ally and notice how the entire landscape now reflects greater harmony and wellness. Walk back to your sanctuary, carrying with you the energy of healing and renewal.

Take several deep breaths and slowly return to ordinary consciousness, knowing that the healing work you've done in imagination is real and will continue to influence your wellbeing in physical reality.

Imaginatio represents nothing less than humanity's divine inheritance - the creative power through which consciousness explores and shapes reality itself. When we learn to work consciously with this faculty, we step into our role as active participants in the ongoing creation of reality rather than passive recipients of whatever circumstances befall us.

The ancient mystery schools understood this truth and created elaborate systems for training students in the sacred art of conscious imagination. Today, we have the opportunity to reclaim this knowledge, integrating ancient wisdom with modern understanding to develop our imaginative faculties for healing, growth, and service to the greater good.

Your imagination is not separate from the divine creative force that brought universes into being - it is your personal participation in that cosmic creativity. Use it wisely, use it consciously, and use it in service of love. Through the power of *Imaginatio*, you have the capacity to heal yourself and your world, one image at a time.

A Mantra for Sacred Imagination

"I am the conscious creator of my inner world. My inner visions serve the highest good, contributing to my own transformation and the evolution of all consciousness."

Further Reading:

Robert A. Johnson: *Inner Work* (on Active Imagination)

Neville Goddard: *The Power of Awareness*

Daskalos (Dr. Stylianos Atteshlis): *Esoteric Practices*

Carl G. Jung: *The Red Book*

Michael Harner: *The Way of the Shaman*

Chapter 7: Frequency

The Art of Conscious Resonance

"If you want to find the secrets to the Universe, think in terms of energy, frequency and vibration." – Nikola Tesla

In the vast symphony of existence, each of us operates as both a broadcasting station and a sensitive receiver, constantly transmitting and receiving the subtle energies of thoughts and emotions. Our personal frequency—the vibrational quality of our being—determines not only what we broadcast into the world but also what we attract and receive from it. Understanding and mastering this frequency is perhaps one of the most practical and transformative skills we can develop in our journey toward conscious living.

The Human Frequency Generator

Every thought we think, every emotion we feel, every intention we hold creates a specific vibrational pattern that radiates outward like ripples on a pond. Modern science confirms what ancient wisdom traditions have long understood: consciousness itself is vibrational in nature. Our brains generate measurable electromagnetic fields, our hearts produce the strongest electromagnetic field in the body, and our entire being operates as a complex frequency generator, constantly broadcasting our inner state to the world around us.

This broadcasting happens whether we're conscious of it or not. Like a radio station that never goes off the air, we are continuously transmitting our frequency through our thoughts, emotions, words, and actions. The quality of this transmission—whether it's broadcasting fear or love, scarcity or abundance, chaos or peace—determines the nature of our lived experience and the type of people and circumstances we attract into our lives.

Simultaneously, we function as highly sensitive receivers, constantly picking up the frequencies of others around us. Have you ever walked into a room and immediately sensed tension, even though nothing was being said? Or found yourself feeling inexplicably uplifted in the presence of certain people? These experiences demonstrate our natural capacity to perceive and be influenced by the frequencies emanating from others.

The Architecture of Thought and Emotion Forms

To truly understand how frequency works, we must delve into the nature of thought forms and emotion forms—the subtle energy structures that our mental and emotional states create. This understanding has been extensively explored by several remarkable researchers and spiritual scientists whose work provides crucial insights into the mechanics of consciousness.

The Insights of Daskalos

Stylianos Atteshlis, known to his students as Daskalos, was a Cypriot mystic and healer whose teachings on the nature of thought forms revolutionized our understanding of consciousness. Through decades of direct observation and experience, Daskalos mapped the subtle anatomy of human consciousness with scientific precision.

According to Daskalos, every thought we think creates a distinct energetic form that continues to exist even after the thought has passed from our conscious awareness. These thought forms are not mere metaphors but actual energetic structures that can be perceived, studied, and worked with. They possess their own momentum and magnetic properties, attracting similar thoughts and circumstances that match their vibrational frequency.

Daskalos taught that thought forms fall into several categories. Constructive thought forms, generated through love, compassion, and positive intention, carry high-frequency vibrations that uplift both the creator and anyone who comes into contact with them. Destructive thought forms, born from fear, anger, jealousy, or hatred, vibrate at lower frequencies and create disturbances in both the individual's energy field and the broader environment.

What makes this understanding particularly powerful is Daskalos's insight that thought forms are not static. They can be consciously transformed through the application of love, understanding, and forgiveness. This means that even deeply ingrained patterns of negative thinking can be healed and transformed when we learn to work skillfully with the frequency of our consciousness.

Rudolf Steiner's Spiritual Science

Rudolf Steiner, the Austrian philosopher and founder of Anthroposophy, provided another crucial perspective on the relationship between consciousness and frequency. Steiner's clairvoyant investigations revealed that human beings exist within multiple interpenetrating bodies of consciousness, each operating at different frequencies.

Steiner described how our thoughts create lasting impressions in what he called the "etheric body"—the life force field that surrounds and interpenetrates our physical form. These impressions, accumulated over time, shape our personal frequency signature and determine our capacity to perceive and interact with different levels of reality.

In Steiner's understanding, the quality of our thinking directly influences our spiritual evolution. Clear, loving thoughts strengthen our connection to higher frequencies and expand our consciousness, while confused, fearful, or selfish thinking creates distortions in our energy field that limit our perception and keep us trapped in lower vibrational states.

Steiner emphasized that developing what he called "pure thinking"—thoughts free from personal desire and ego-driven motivation—was essential for spiritual development. This pure thinking naturally resonates at higher frequencies and opens us to wisdom, inspiration, and connection with the deeper currents of life.

Charles Leadbeater's Clairvoyant Research

Charles W. Leadbeater, a member of the Theosophical Society and gifted clairvoyant, made detailed observations of how thoughts and emotions appear to supersensible perception. His book "Thought-Forms," co-authored with Annie Besant, provides vivid descriptions of the colors, shapes, and movements that different types of thoughts and emotions create in the subtle dimensions.

Leadbeater observed that emotions create particularly powerful forms, often appearing as swirling clouds of color around individuals. Love manifests as beautiful rose-colored forms that expand outward and uplift everything they touch. Anger appears as jagged red flashes that create disturbance and discord. Fear generates gray, shadowy forms that seem to compress and contract the energy field.

What's remarkable about Leadbeater's observations is how they correlate with modern research on emotional states and their physiological effects. The expansion and coherence he observed in loving states matches what contemporary science has discovered about the heart's electromagnetic field during states of appreciation and care.

Leadbeater also noted that thoughts and emotions of similar frequency naturally attract and reinforce each other. A person dwelling in fearful thoughts tends to attract more fear-based experiences, while someone maintaining thoughts of love and gratitude draws similar energies into their field of experience.

The Practice of Conscious Check-In

Given the constant activity of our thought and emotion generating system, developing a regular practice of "checking in" with our current frequency becomes essential. This practice involves pausing throughout the day to assess our current vibrational state and making conscious adjustments when needed.

The check-in process begins with simple awareness. We ask ourselves: "What is my frequency right now? What am I broadcasting into the world through my thoughts, emotions, and overall energy?" This isn't about judgment or criticism, but about honest assessment with the aim of conscious course correction.

Often, we discover that we've been running unconscious programs—habitual patterns of thinking and feeling that operate below the threshold of awareness. We might find ourselves caught in worry loops about future events, replaying past hurts, or simply operating on automatic pilot without any conscious direction of our energy.

The beauty of the check-in practice is that awareness itself begins to shift our frequency. The moment we become conscious of a low-frequency state, we create space for choice. We're no longer completely identified with the pattern; instead, we become the observer of it, which immediately raises our vibrational level.

A simple check-in protocol might involve:

Physical Assessment: How does my body feel right now? Am I tense, relaxed, energized, or depleted? The body often reflects our emotional and mental frequency more accurately than our conscious mind.

Emotional Scanning: What emotions are present in this moment? Am I feeling contracted or expanded, heavy or light, resistant or flowing?

Mental Observation: What kinds of thoughts have been cycling through my mind? Are they constructive or destructive, future-focused worries or present-moment awareness?

Energetic Sensing: If I imagine my overall energy as a color or musical tone, what would it be? This intuitive assessment often provides immediate feedback about our current frequency.

The "How Would I Feel If..." Technique

One of the most powerful tools for consciously shifting frequency is the "How would I feel if..." technique. This method works by engaging our imagination to experience the emotional and energetic state associated with our desired outcome before it manifests in external reality.

The technique operates on the principle that our nervous system and energy field respond to vividly imagined experiences almost as powerfully as they do to actual events. By mentally rehearsing the feeling state of our desired reality, we begin to broadcast that frequency and attract circumstances that match it.

The practice begins by identifying a specific outcome or state we wish to experience. Rather than focusing on the external circumstances, we dive directly into the feeling of having already achieved it. We ask ourselves: "How would I feel if this were already true? How would I move through the world? How would I treat others? What would be different about my energy?"

For example, instead of worrying about a challenging work presentation, we might practice feeling confident, prepared, and excited about sharing our knowledge. Instead of dwelling in anxiety about a relationship conflict, we could embody the feeling of resolution, understanding, and renewed connection.

The key is to make these feeling states as vivid and real as possible. We don't just think about feeling confident; we actually generate the bodily sensations, emotional tone, and mental clarity that confidence brings. We practice walking, speaking, and breathing from that state until it becomes a familiar frequency we can access at will.

This technique is particularly powerful because it breaks us out of the limiting pattern of trying to feel better by changing external circumstances. Instead, we recognize that we can choose our frequency first, and then watch as external reality shifts to match our new vibrational state.

Regular practice with this technique develops what we might call "frequency flexibility"—the ability to consciously shift our vibrational state regardless of current circumstances. This skill becomes invaluable during challenging times when external conditions might otherwise pull us into lower frequencies.

Creating Your Personal Frequency Enhancement Collection

Just as musicians develop a repertoire of pieces they can play, conscious frequency workers benefit from cultivating a personal collection of images, memories, practices, and experiences that reliably elevate their vibrational state. This collection serves as a resource we can draw upon whenever we need to shift from a lower to a higher frequency.

Building this collection requires paying attention to what genuinely moves and uplifts you, not what you think should work or what works for others. The most powerful frequency shifters are deeply personal and connect with your unique emotional and spiritual landscape.

Visual Imagery: Collect mental images that instantly shift your energy. This might be a breathtaking sunset you once witnessed, the face of someone you love deeply, a sacred place that touches your soul, or even an imagined scene of perfect peace and beauty. Practice visualizing these images with such detail and feeling that they become reliable tools for frequency elevation.

Memory Banks: Identify peak experiences from your life—moments when you felt most alive, connected, joyful, or peaceful. These might be times of spiritual communion, experiences of unconditional love, moments of perfect flow in creative work, or instances of profound connection with nature. Practice returning to these memories not just mentally but energetically, allowing yourself to re-experience the frequency they generated.

Emotional Anchors: Notice which emotions most effectively raise your frequency. For some people, gratitude is the fastest elevator to higher states. Others find that compassion, wonder, determination, or playfulness work most effectively. Practice generating these emotions independent of external circumstances, building your capacity to access them at will.

Somatic Practices: Identify physical movements, breathing patterns, or postures that shift your energy. This might be a particular yoga pose, a way of moving your arms, a specific breathing rhythm, or even a way of holding your facial features. The body is a powerful frequency generator, and small physical shifts can create dramatic changes in our overall vibrational state.

Sensory Triggers: Notice which sensory experiences reliably uplift you. The scent of roses, the sound of ocean waves, the feel of silk, the taste of fresh mint—all of these can serve as instant frequency shifters when consciously employed.

The Science of Heart Coherence

The work of the HeartMath® Institute has provided crucial scientific validation for many traditional teachings about frequency and consciousness. Their research demonstrates that the heart generates the strongest electromagnetic field in the human body—a field that extends several feet beyond our physical form and can be measured by sensitive instruments.

Even more remarkable is their discovery that the heart's electromagnetic field changes dramatically based on our emotional state. During states of appreciation, care, and love, the heart generates what they term "coherent" patterns—smooth, ordered, harmonious rhythms that indicate optimal function. During states of stress, frustration, or anxiety, the heart produces "incoherent" patterns—jagged, chaotic rhythms that indicate dysfunction.

This coherence or incoherence doesn't remain isolated to the individual. HeartMath® research has shown that people in close proximity can actually synchronize their heart rhythms, especially when one person maintains a coherent state. This provides scientific evidence for what sensitive people have always known: our emotional and energetic states directly influence those around us.

The HeartMath® Institute has developed specific techniques for generating heart coherence, including:

Heart-Focused Breathing: Directing attention to the heart area while breathing at a slower, more rhythmic pace (approximately five seconds in, five seconds out). This simple practice begins to shift heart rhythm patterns toward coherence.

Activation of Heart Feelings: While maintaining heart-focused breathing, consciously activating feelings of appreciation, care, or compassion. This combination of focused attention and positive emotion creates optimal heart coherence patterns.

Sustained Appreciation: Identifying something or someone you genuinely appreciate and focusing on that appreciation while maintaining heart-centered breathing. This practice not only generates coherence but also creates lasting shifts in your overall frequency.

Cultivating the Inner Observer

Perhaps the most crucial skill in frequency mastery is developing what spiritual traditions call the "witness consciousness" or "inner observer." This is the part of awareness that can step back from our thoughts and emotions and observe them without being completely identified with them.

Most of us live in a state of unconscious identification with our mental and emotional activity. When we're angry, we become the anger. When we're worried, we become the worry. When we're joyful, we become the joy. This total identification means we have no choice in our frequency—we're simply at the mercy of whatever thoughts and emotions arise.

The inner observer changes this dynamic completely. When we can observe our anger without becoming it, we maintain choice about how to respond. When we can witness our worry without being consumed by it, we preserve our capacity for clear thinking and wise action. When we can be aware of our joy without clinging to it, we can appreciate it fully without the anxiety of trying to make it permanent.

Developing the inner observer requires consistent practice. Traditional meditation is one of the most effective ways to strengthen this capacity, as it trains us to observe the constant stream of mental and emotional activity without being swept away by it.

Labeling Practice: Throughout the day, practice simply labeling what you observe in your mental and emotional landscape. "I notice worry arising." "I'm aware of feeling frustrated." "I see thoughts about the future spinning." This simple act of labeling creates distance between you and the experience, awakening the observer.

Physical Awareness: Use your body as an anchor for observer consciousness. Regularly check in with physical sensations—the feeling of your feet on the ground, your breathing, the temperature of the air on your skin. This practice grounds you in present-moment awareness and strengthens your capacity to observe without reaction.

Emotional Weather Reports: Practice describing your emotional state as if you were giving a weather report. "There's a storm of anxiety moving through right now." "I'm experiencing some cloudy thinking with occasional bursts of clarity." This metaphorical approach helps maintain the observer perspective while acknowledging what's present.

Recognizing the Moment of Choice: Learn to recognize the moment between stimulus and response—the instant when you can choose how to react to whatever is arising. This choice point is where your power lives, and recognizing it consistently is a sign that your inner observer is becoming stronger.

The inner observer doesn't eliminate difficult thoughts and emotions; instead, it provides space around them. In this space, you can make conscious choices about your frequency rather than being unconsciously driven by whatever arises in your mental and emotional landscape.

Environmental Frequency Factors

While we have significant control over our internal frequency through conscious practice, it's important to acknowledge that external factors also influence our vibrational state. Understanding and working skillfully with these environmental influences is part of taking full responsibility for our frequency.

Natural Environments: Most people experience an immediate frequency shift when they spend time in nature. The electromagnetic fields of trees, the negative ions generated by moving water, the fractal patterns found in natural forms—all of these contribute to raising human frequency. Regular time in natural settings isn't just pleasant; it's a necessary component of maintaining optimal vibrational health.

Architectural Spaces: The spaces we inhabit significantly influence our frequency. High ceilings, natural light, clean lines, and harmonious proportions tend to uplift our energy, while cluttered, cramped, or poorly lit spaces can drag down our vibrational state. Paying attention to how different environments affect you and making conscious choices about your physical surroundings is part of frequency mastery.

Sound Frequencies: Music, natural sounds, and even the background noise of our environment all influence our frequency. Classical music, particularly pieces written in mathematical ratios that mirror natural harmony, tends to elevate consciousness. Nature sounds like ocean waves, birdsong, or wind through trees often induce calm, coherent states. Conversely, harsh, discordant, or excessively loud sounds can disrupt our energy field and pull down our frequency.

Human Company: The people we spend time with perhaps have the most significant environmental impact on our frequency. As the HeartMath® research demonstrates, we naturally synchronize with the electromagnetic fields of those around us. Spending time with people who maintain high-frequency states through practices like gratitude, compassion, and conscious awareness tends to elevate our own frequency. Conversely, prolonged exposure to people operating from fear, anger, or unconscious reactivity can pull down our vibrational state.

Media and Information: In our information-saturated world, what we choose to read, watch, and listen to significantly impacts our frequency. News media, with its focus on conflict and crisis, often generates fear-based frequencies. Social media can trap us in comparison and inadequacy. Consciously choosing uplifting, inspiring, and educational content is part of taking responsibility for our vibrational environment.

Sensory Inputs: Simple sensory experiences can be powerful frequency shifters. The scent of essential oils, the feeling of soft fabrics, the taste of pure water, the sight of beautiful art—all of these can instantly shift our vibrational state when consciously employed.

The key is developing sensitivity to how these environmental factors affect you personally and then making conscious choices about your exposure. This doesn't mean avoiding all challenging environments, but rather maintaining awareness of their impact and taking proactive steps to maintain your desired frequency.

Taking Responsibility for Your Broadcast

As Gandhi wisely observed, we must "be the change we want to see in the world." In frequency terms, this means taking complete responsibility for what we're broadcasting through our thoughts, emotions, words, and actions. Every moment, we're contributing to the collective human frequency, either adding to the fear, division, and unconsciousness in the world or contributing to the love, unity, and awakening that humanity desperately needs.

This responsibility begins with honest self-assessment. What am I actually broadcasting most of the time? Am I contributing to solutions or problems? Am I adding to the beauty and harmony in the world or increasing the chaos and discord? These questions require courage to answer honestly, but they're essential for conscious evolution.

Taking responsibility doesn't mean achieving perfection or never having challenging thoughts and emotions. It means becoming increasingly conscious of our inner states and making consistent efforts to align our frequency with our highest values and aspirations.

Conscious Communication: Pay attention to how you speak with others. Are your words uplifting, encouraging, and constructive, or do they tend toward criticism, complaining, and negativity? The frequency of our communication has enormous impact on both ourselves and others.

Emotional Hygiene: Just as we practice physical hygiene to maintain health, we need emotional and mental hygiene practices to maintain frequency. This includes regularly clearing accumulated negative emotions, releasing resentments, and consciously generating positive emotional states. Sometimes this will require a healthy dose of self-forgiveness.

Service and Contribution: One of the most powerful ways to maintain high frequency is to focus on how you can serve and contribute to others' wellbeing. When we shift from "what can I get?" to "what can I give?" our frequency naturally rises to match this more expansive orientation.

Integrity Alignment: Living in alignment with your deepest values and authentic nature generates coherent, high-frequency states. When there's a gap between who you really are and how you're living, it creates internal discord that lowers your vibrational state.

Becoming the Radio Station You Want to Listen To

This brings us to a fundamental reframe of Gandhi's teaching: be the radio station that you want to listen to. If you could tune into the broadcast of your own consciousness, would you want to keep listening? Would the content be inspiring, uplifting, and wise, or would it be repetitive loops of worry, complaint, and unconscious reactivity?

This metaphor helps us understand the full implications of frequency work. We're not just trying to feel better for our own sake (though that's certainly valuable). We're recognizing that our personal frequency is our contribution to the collective human field. In a world desperately needing more love, wisdom, and conscious awareness, every person who commits to maintaining a high-frequency broadcast is performing a service to all life.

Imagine a world where even a significant minority of people took responsibility for their frequency. Imagine communities where most individuals practiced regular check-ins, conscious frequency elevation, and emotional hygiene. Imagine families, schools, and workplaces operating from coherent, heart-centered states rather than reactive, fear-based patterns.

This isn't utopian fantasy; it's the natural result of individuals taking responsibility for their own vibrational state and recognizing the profound impact this has on everything around them. Your personal frequency work is simultaneously the most selfish and most selfless thing you can do—selfish because it dramatically improves your own life experience, and selfless because it contributes to the healing and elevation of our entire world.

The path forward requires commitment, consistency, and compassion—commitment to the ongoing work of frequency mastery, consistency in practicing the tools and techniques that maintain high-vibrational states, and compassion for yourself and others during the inevitable moments when frequency drops.

Remember that mastering frequency is not about maintaining perpetual bliss or never experiencing challenging emotions. It's about developing the skill to consciously choose your vibrational state regardless of circumstances, and to quickly return to coherent, loving frequencies when you've been knocked off course by life's inevitable challenges.

As you continue this journey, you join a growing community of conscious individuals who understand that personal transformation and planetary transformation are inseparable. Every moment you spend in practices that elevate your frequency, every choice you make to broadcast love rather than fear, every time you serve as a beacon of coherent awareness in a chaotic world—these are not small personal achievements but contributions to the greatest work of our time: the conscious evolution of human consciousness itself.

In the end, frequency mastery is both a science and an art, both a personal practice and a planetary service. It requires understanding the mechanics of how thoughts and emotions create vibrational patterns, while also cultivating the sensitivity and wisdom to work skillfully with these subtle energies. It demands both the precision of a scientist and the heart of a poet, both the discipline of a dedicated practitioner and the playfulness of an eternal student.

Your frequency is your signature in the symphony of existence. Make it a melody that uplifts not only your own soul but contributes to the harmony of the whole. Be the radio station that broadcast love, wisdom, and conscious awareness—because the world is listening, and it desperately needs your unique contribution to the healing and awakening of all life.

Exercise 1: The Frequency Check-In Practice

Set a gentle alarm to go off three times throughout your day at random intervals. When it sounds, pause whatever you're doing and ask yourself these four questions:

1. **Physical**: How does my body feel right now? Tense, relaxed, energized, depleted?

2. **Emotional**: What emotions are present? Am I contracted or expanded, heavy or light?

3. **Mental**: What thoughts have been cycling through my mind? Are they constructive or destructive?

4. **Energetic**: If my overall energy were a color or musical note, what would it be?

Don't judge what you find—just notice. If you discover you're broadcasting frustration, worry, or negativity, simply acknowledge it with the same compassion you'd show a friend having a rough day. This awareness alone often begins to shift your frequency naturally.

Note: If you find yourself consistently in low-frequency states, consider whether external factors (news consumption, certain relationships, work stress) might need attention, or whether speaking with a counselor could be helpful.

Exercise 2: The "Upgrade Your Broadcast" Technique

When you catch yourself in a low-frequency state, try this simple reset:

1. **Pause and breathe** three slow, deep breaths

2. **Ask yourself**: "How would I feel if everything in my life was working out perfectly?"

3. **Generate that feeling** in your body for 30 seconds—not the circumstances, just the emotional frequency

4. **Carry that feeling** into whatever you do next, like wearing an invisible cloak of possibility

Think of it like tuning a radio from static to your favorite station. You're not denying current challenges; you're consciously choosing which frequency to broadcast while you handle them. Sometimes the best thing you can offer a difficult situation is your highest frequency rather than matching its chaos.

Prompt 1: Your Frequency Autobiography

Write about a time when you were in your highest frequency—when you felt most alive, connected, and authentic. What were the circumstances? Who were you with? What had you been doing or thinking about? Most importantly, what did that frequency feel like in your body, and how did it affect the people around you?

Now contrast this with a time when you were broadcasting from fear, anger, or despair. What external factors contributed to each state? What patterns do you notice about what elevates or depletes your frequency? Be specific.

Prompt 2: The People Who Change Your Channel

Make two lists: people who consistently raise your frequency and those who tend to lower it. For the frequency-raisers, write about what qualities they possess or express that uplifts you. For the frequency-drainers, consider whether they're dealing with their own challenges or if there are boundary issues to address.

This isn't about judging others, but about becoming conscious of how different relationships affect your energetic state. Sometimes we can learn to maintain our frequency around challenging people; sometimes we need to limit exposure while they work through their own patterns.

Prompt 3: Your Environmental Energy Audit

Take a walk through your living space, workplace, or daily routine with "frequency eyes." What environments, objects, sounds, or activities consistently make you feel more alive and centered? What consistently makes you feel drained, scattered, or agitated?

Write about creating an action plan for increasing exposure to frequency-raising environments and minimizing time in frequency-draining ones. Remember, sometimes we can't change our environment immediately, but we can change how we relate to it.

Prompt 4: Broadcasting Love in a Fear-Based World

Imagine you're a radio station in a city full of static and negativity. What would your "programming" look like? How would you maintain signal strength without becoming preachy or disconnected from real struggles? Write about how you might broadcast hope, compassion, and wisdom while still acknowledging the genuine challenges people face. Use your voice. What are the things that lie closest to your heart?

Consider: What would it mean to be a healing presence in your family, workplace, or community without trying to fix everyone or becoming a doormat?

Mantra

"I choose my frequency consciously. My inner peace is my gift to the world."

Further Reading:

C.W.Leadbeater &Annie Besant: *Thought Forms*

C.W.Leadbeater: *Man Visible and Invisible*

Mitch Horowitz: *The Miracle Club*

G. Epstein M.D& B.Fedoroff, Editors: *The Encyclopedia of Mental Imagery*

In Closing

I could sum up the concepts of this book in the following image: Have the courage to steer your ship towards unknown waters, face any storms with courage, don't let the pirates board your ship, bring along some mates to keep you company, remember to dream under the stars, and make sure you send out helpful signals to other boats in your vicinity when you discover new treasures. We are on a journey, and great ships were built for great voyages.

Fair winds!

Remember: Working with all of these inner qualities and strengths isn't about forced positivity or spiritual bypassing. It's about taking conscious responsibility for the energy you contribute to the world while remaining authentic to your human experience. Be patient with yourself as you develop these practices—like learning any new skill, it takes time and gentle persistence. And occasionally the ability to laugh at yourself.

About the Author

Adrienne Prince has spent over 45 years exploring mystical and wisdom traditions from both East and West—from Taoist and Renaissance alchemy to Gnosticism, Kabbalah, and Christian esoteric practices. It's been a long and winding journey, but she wouldn't have it any other way.

Growing up across four European countries and studying at the University of Florence gave her a deep appreciation for how different cultures approach life's bigger questions. Those years shaped her enduring fascination with philosophy, spirituality, and the rich currents of Mediterranean wisdom traditions.

As a certified holistic counselor, astrologer, and workshop leader, she now helps others navigate their own paths of self-discovery. She's also an avid photographer and mixed-media artist, bringing a creative sensibility to her work with active imagination and visualization techniques.

Through writing and teaching, Adrienne's aim is straightforward: to bridge ancient wisdom and contemporary tools for consciousness expansion, and to make these tools accessible, relevant and interesting. Because exploring the depths doesn't have to mean taking yourself too seriously along the way.

www.ingramcontent.com/pod-product-compliance
Lightning Source LLC
Chambersburg PA
CBHW051537120626
46551CB00012B/1262